QUANTUM
ORGANIZING

QUANTUM ORGANIZING

Clearing the Path
to Personal and Professional Success

LINDA WILLIAMS

Accelerator Books

Accelerator Books
P.O. Box 1241
Princeton, NJ 08542
www.acceleratorbooks.com

Editing by Heidi Schreiner.
Cover and Interior Text Design by Eve Siegel.
Typesetting by Rainbow Graphics.

ISBN: 978-0-9815245-2-8

Printed in the United States of America.

Acknowledgments

Of the many people who have been instrumental in bringing *Quantum Organizing* to life, I would especially like to thank Gemma Farrell for her guidance and support through the intricacies of publishing, Heidi von Schreiner for her help with the many aspects of editing and pulling everything together, and my friends and family who provided helpful encouragement, comments, and even a few anecdotes.

Contents

QUANTUM
ORGANIZING

CHAPTER 1

Why Quantum Organizing Works

Create your own universe as you go along.
—Winston Churchill

All that we are is what we have thought.
—Buddha

Three Rules of Work: Out of clutter find simplicity; From discord find harmony; In the middle of difficulty lies opportunity.
—Albert Einstein

On television shows that discuss how to get organized, such as *Organize This*, *Clean House*, and *Extreme Home Makeover*, by the end of the program, families are transformed. The overworked mother suddenly has time to play board games with her children. The retiree who couldn't fit his car inside his garage because it was so cluttered now has plenty of space around his new garage workbench to pursue his hobbies. Fathers are playing ball with the kids after work instead of cleaning up inside. Teenagers suddenly have no problem making it to school on time now that they don't have to wade through an island of laundry to find something to wear. You can see the weight peel off the faces of these folks; their smiles are brighter. Simply being able to see the floor of your closet can change your entire self-image and improve your life in unforeseen ways. By clearing out the clutter in your life, you make room for more positive energy to flow. And that can generate dynamic change in multiple areas. It is not uncommon for my newly organized clients to find that suddenly they are back in school, changing careers, losing weight, or improving their relationships. Is it really possible that something as basic as an orderly home can be so life-changing? It absolutely is, and *Quantum Organizing* will show you how.

As you delve into these pages, you probably will notice that the quantum method is quite different from other organizing systems you may know. My system is built on the premise that there is more to organizing a home than simply buying color-coded containers. I believe that even if you remove every ounce of clutter from your home, you will never be truly organized until you also improve the energy in your space. An organized room not only helps you to accomplish tasks easily, but it also supports you spiritually. When you are done reworking your rooms, you should feel not only tidier but also more confident and centered as well. Before you remove even one knickknack, you will have an entire quantum plan in place for your room so that the completed space will leave you and your loved ones energized and in charge. Eventually we will get out the boxes, but the process that leads up to paring down a space is equally important. You see, it really is mind over matter! Once you approach a space with a clear end goal in mind, the sorting and packing up become a piece of cake. Reorganizing never should feel like a burden. Positive change is exciting, and kicking out the clutter should be exhilarating as well. You are on your way to reaching your full potential, perhaps for the very first time.

Today people use the term *quantum leap* to describe a great jump forward, a revolutionary advance. Certainly organizing a home can be revolutionary for many people. In physics, a quantum leap is a very small but instantaneous change that occurs when an electron makes a jump from one energy state to another within an atom. Everything in our world is composed of energy-filled atoms, including people and the homes they live in. People often talk about a place having negative or positive energy without really comprehending what is meant by the term. The emotional state of the people inside a space can change the reality of the space. Our emotions have a direct impact on the areas we inhabit. And when we feel positive and energized, our homes become positive places to be. The reverse is equally true. When a space is clean and orderly, we feel more positive when we are in it. This is why the first step to organizing a room is to clarify your thinking about that space. *Quantum Organizing* will lead you step by step through the process of envisioning your perfect space so that you will be able to create it easily. Next, *Quantum Organizing* will show you how to remove your clutter and reorganize. More quickly than you can imagine, the room that you have been dreaming about will become a reality. And once you are living in a space that supports you properly, your whole life will brighten. I know this for a fact because I have seen it happen for my clients hundreds of times.

As an efficiency expert and an industrial engineer, I have spent twenty years planning and implementing organizational changes for large corporations. My job is to help departments become more effective. The changes I institute are, for the most part, commonsense measures. For example, I have cut down on the wait time to see doctors in hospitals by ensuring that there are extra admitting clerks working during peak hours. I have helped human resources departments dispatch calls more speedily by redesigning their filing systems so that the reference materials they need are close at hand. I have helped payroll departments get paychecks out on time by automating their data input. Given the time and the resources, these employees perhaps could have found similar solutions on their own. But having a set of expert eyes trained on a problem definitely speeds up the process and improves the results. In *Quantum Organizing*, I help you apply these same techniques to your home life. Once your home is functioning well, you will be amazed at what a burden is lifted from your shoulders. Home once again will be the place you most want to be.

One trick efficiency experts learn is to analyze the gap between a company's current performance and its true potential. We use sophisticated research models to determine how much a company produces and compare this amount with the business's maximum potential. Once we have determined what a company is ideally capable of achieving, we help our clients to bridge the gap between where they are and where they can be. Clients frequently are amazed at the positive impact these simple organizational changes can have. In addition to saving the corporation money, getting organized benefits customers as well. When I organize a patient intake system for a large hospital, for example, the hospital can maximize the number of patients treated per hour. Patients get the care they need more quickly, so they win too. It is really satisfying to see workplaces improve.

Now I am applying these same skills that I have honed as a corporate efficiency expert to my individual clients. After all, most families are run in ways that are not dissimilar to a small business. Any parent can tell you this. It's even more rewarding to see families bridge their "gap" and reach their full potential. Although these changes are happening on a smaller canvas, they are every bit as transforming for those involved. But there are so many more families in need of help! These are the people that I had in mind when I decided to write *Quantum Organizing*. This book clearly outlines all the steps you need to take in order to achieve positive changes in your own home.

Of course, a home is not exactly like a business. Your home is your sanctuary, too, and it needs to be not only productive but also supportive. A well-run home nourishes the people who live there, both materially and spiritually. In addition to giving important tips and information on how to make your home more efficient, *Quantum Organizing* also delves into the spiritual aspects of your space. Each chapter includes important tips and uplifting information based on the ancient Chinese art of Feng Shui and the power of the laws of attraction. What's an engineer like me doing dabbling in these metaphysical ideologies? To my mind, they just make good common sense. When your heart and mind are in the right place, everything else falls into line. You don't have to believe in Feng Shui or the laws of attraction to use this book. Whether you choose to practice Feng Shui or not, you can still follow the steps in *Quantum Organizing* and create a clean, orderly home. But if you are ready to try something new, I encourage you to visualize a purpose for each of your rooms (laws of attraction; see below) and incorporate your vision of the space into your floor plan (Feng Shui). If you do, you may find that the results you achieve resonate with your family on a deeper level. Later on, I will explain exactly how these important beliefs play a role in organizing one's home. For now, it is enough to know that clearing the clutter out of your space will leave you not only more organized but also more content. The "elbow grease" that uncluttering requires pays for itself many times over and benefits your life on multiple levels.

Although I currently work for a large Fortune 500 company, moving from the corporate arena into the personal organizing sphere has been a natural transition for me. Whether there are five thousand employees in your space or five, the same rules apply. I still get a little buzz every time I see a way to solve an organizational challenge. I think I am just an organizer at heart. Call me compulsive, but I can tell you that my life is considerably less frantic as a result. I always arrive on time, with my mascara in my bag just where it belongs. As a kid, I always had the neat-est drawers! As a teenager, I created my first work flowchart. I had separate notebooks for each of my classes plus a master list for homework to-dos. That was the beginning of my love of lists! I love lists, and I continue to use lists to track what needs to be done. In graduate school, I worked as a server in the dining hall. It used to make me crazy to hear the same questions thirty times a night: "What's the special?" "Where's the ketchup?" "Where do the trays go?" "Is there any more butter?" I couldn't help myself. I labeled all the supply shelves for the staff, reorganized the condi-ments, and posted a schedule showing the specials. I transformed that dining hall into a model of efficiency, leaving diners free to focus on friends and servers to focus on serving them. As a young, single mother of a toddler, I laid out my daughter's clothes and the bag for the sitter the evening before. When the morning rush came, it was easy to fix breakfast, dress my daughter, and hit the road to get to my job by seven o'clock.

These were some of my tricks, and I am sure you have a few of your own too. One thing I have learned working with both companies and individuals is that there is no one-size-fits-all solution. Many professional organizers overlook the individual in their rush to sort things out. This book is designed to take your unique individuality into account. It aims to help you identify the very best ways for you to sort out your space, whether you're a sentimentalist who likes to keep small items of inspiration in view or a purist who sleeps better at night knowing that there is not a cup or vase cluttering your tabletops. As with dieting, there are myriad approaches you can take, and what works well for your neighbor may not suit you.

In fact, one of my favorite things about personal organizing is seeing the task of organizing from different perspectives and finding a formula that fits my clients' unique personalities. I recently worked with a minimalist whose "stuff" had become overwhelming. "Serene and Green" was her mantra. She wanted to walk into her small condo and see nothing but clean, clear space and lush, green plants. Together we focused on what she really wanted, which was to build an imaginary fence around her living room. We relocated her books and magazines to her office, on the other side of the "fence." Personally, I like a few books and magazines around, but that's not her thing, and we needed to make her living space work for her. In the end, what we created allowed this client to realize a genuine sense of harmony with her surroundings, which let her reclaim her energy for her highest purpose. I had another client who previously had lived in Europe and had collected many cherished antique paintings, pieces of furniture, and tabletop items. When we organized her space, we made a plan that included a special spot to display each one of her treasures because seeing these items on a daily basis grounded her. Whatever your personality, I promise that once you take the first significant steps toward order, you will find that your entire life will change.

Truly effective personal organizing involves so much more than just a system of neat piles and detailed lists. At its core, *Quantum Organizing* is about achieving harmony with your environment. The ancient Chinese art of Feng Shui is one of the principles that I include in my quantum toolbox of tricks. Feng Shui has been practiced for centuries, and it gives very specific guidelines on how to arrange a space. I first practiced Feng Shui under a renown Feng Shui master, and what I learned under his tutelage was life-changing. I believe that I have a much more complete understanding of harmony and balance as a result of my studies, and I am excited to share what I have learned with you in this book. It was my studies of Feng Shui and other philosophies that led me to create the idea of quantum organizing, which combines science and philosophy to form a wholly unique and holistic approach to housekeeping.

Feng Shui's basic premise is that everything in the universe, animate and inanimate, either facilitates or blocks *chi*. *Chi* translates literally as "air" or "breath" and refers to the flow of energy. It's what Westerners commonly call "spirit" or "life force." *Chi* flows through your home and your life like water. You can live harmoniously in a place where the energy, or *chi*, flows freely, or you can struggle through life in surroundings where the flow of energy is blocked by piles of stuff. When you try to put more water into an already full cup, it overflows, and the water is wasted. If your furniture is awkwardly arranged, if mounds of junk crowd your hallway, if clothes cover your bed, or if your desk is buried in clutter, *chi* cannot flow freely, and the positive energy is lost. The way we organize our living spaces can either facilitate the flow of positive energy or cause it to stagnate. When you live in a home where the *chi* is blocked, you will feel emotionally blocked and out of sorts as well. Feng Shui masters believe that your outer environment both reflects and affects your inner self. Discord within can generates chaotic surroundings, and the reverse is also true: Chaotic surroundings create inner discord.

The Eastern concept of *chi* has its expression in modern Western science as well. Twentieth-century physics, also called *quantum physics*, is based on the discovery that subatomic particles behave like waves. Since all matter is made up of subatomic particles, a solid object, such as a chair or a stack of newspapers, is actually a collection of wavelike energy that is dense enough to appear solid. Although quantum theory has been poked and prodded plenty by scientists, it remains the best explanation we have to date of how microscopic atoms behave. People are also made up of atoms, and so the principles of quantum theory apply to us as well. If everything has and in fact is energy, then we have a choice. We can either facilitate the flow of positive energy or allow it to be stymied and mired in negativity.

This brings me to the last important principle that I'd like to discuss. The idea has been around for centuries but has recently experienced a renaissance via the media, including programs such as *Oprah* and in books and movies such as *The Secret*. It is the law of attraction. It's a simple concept with profound applications. At its core, the law of attraction posits that energy flows where your attention goes. In other words, thoughts create things. We create our own universes, and we absolutely have the power to create the solutions to our own problems. The key is to focus on what we want and not on what we don't want. When you focus on the mess in your home, you give energy to the very thing you don't want—the mess. This tells the universe to give you more, and the universe always responds. You actually attract more mess! Instead of dwelling on the lack in your life, you can break the cycle of negativity by asking the universe for what you really want.

Our lives are meant to be abundant and joy-filled. If you really believe this, it will become true for you. In the next chapter I focus on your personal vision of an orderly life and even begin to make that vision a reality. I believe that everyone has the inner power to create his or her ideal environment. If you can believe it too, I assure you that the universe will rearrange itself to make positive things happen for you. Once you visualize your unique space as though it is already perfect, you will find that you have all the energy you need to put the plan into action.

The word *quantum* is Latin for "how much." "How much?" is a question you will be asking yourself again and again as you go through the process of making over your home. How much do I need? How much can I do without? How much will be just enough and yet not too much? How much do I want to change? Striking the right balance will be tricky, but by simply asking the question, you put yourself on the path to quantum change.

CHAPTER 2

Clarifying Your Vision of Your Ideal Space

It is not because things are difficult that we do not dare, it is because we do not dare that they are difficult.

—*Seneca*

You can't depend on your judgment when your imagination is out of focus.
—*Mark Twain*

The problems of the world cannot possibly be solved by skeptics or cynics whose horizons are limited by the obvious realities. We need men who can dream of things that never were.

—*John F. Kennedy*

Jumping Mouse is a Native-American myth. It tells the story of a very generous little mouse who breaks out of his box, so to speak. At first, Jumping Mouse is completely focused on what he needs to do to survive. Like his mice buddies, he is "busy with mouse things." The mice are down in the weeds getting things done, unaware of the forest around them and the mountains above.

But this particular little mouse is intrigued by a great roaring sound he hears. When he asks his fellow mice if they hear the sound, they are too busy to take notice and call him "foolish in the head." The other mice are frozen in their old habits, unable to see beyond their typically cluttered days. Jumping Mouse tries to ignore the sound, but his curiosity gets the best of him. He goes exploring further afield and has a great many adventures. Because he is compassionate toward the larger creatures he meets on his journey, they safely transport him to vistas far beyond the mouse's home. In the end, Jumping Mouse is scooped up by an eagle who carries him high into the sky, and he has the opportunity to see things that all his mouse companions have missed. He discovers that the rushing river is what makes the great roaring sound, and he finally gets a glimpse of the sacred mountain that has become his quest. Jumping Mouse's new vantage point broadens his perspective and gives him wisdom and strength far beyond that of his fellow mice.

When he is held aloft by the eagle, Jumping Mouse sees the "big picture." Like busy mice, our complicated lives force us to spend time a lot of time enmeshed in life's tiny details, living in "mouse view," so to speak. At times, everyone needs the kind of big picture view that Jumping Mouse gets when he is held aloft by the eagle. On some days, even "eagle view" can seem inadequate—we need "space shuttle view"! When organizing a space, it's important to alternate frequently between micro and macro points of view. Eagle view helps you to create a broad vision for an entire area, and mouse view helps you to decide where to keep the spare keys.

The top-down perspective that eagle view affords is essential for creating an overall vision. Does the furniture layout in a particular room work for your family? Will the room function well? Next, you have to open up that overstuffed drawer and start putting its contents in order. This is mouse view. Both views are critical for getting and organized, and they're also both essential for a balanced life.

In this chapter I am going to ask you to concentrate very purposefully, from eagle height, on creating an ideal overall vision of how your home, your room, or your closet should look. We'll also spend some time down in mouse view to ensure that the vision you create will fulfill all your practical needs. Finally, we will zoom back into eagle view. Don't underestimate how powerful an active vision can be. Spend time making the vision so real that it connects through all your senses. If in your mind's eye you can actually touch it, feel it, and taste it, then you will be well on your way to making the vision a reality. When your vision is so real that you feel as if all the positive changes in the space have already taken place, then you will start to see it manifest.

Creating the vision is in many ways your most challenging task. This may seem surprising to you. You may have spent months or even years overwhelmed by your space and its inadequacies. You may think that the greatest challenge lies in dealing with all the mess! But believe it or not, once you can clearly envision what you want your space to look like, changing the space to match your vision is surprisingly simple.

And dealing with the mess turns out to be easier than you think. Imagine that your current mess is a beaver dam in the middle of a pond. Beavers like yourself have been diligently adding logs to this dam for several seasons. The pile is impressively high now, towering over the pond and preventing the water beneath from running its natural course. The water, which represents energy, is now stagnating in pools around the logs. If you study the dam carefully, however, you can see where the water is trapped. You can envision how the stream would flow naturally if the dam were not there. So you move two or three logs. Within minutes, the current builds, and the water surges through and washes the dam downstream. The energy is free to flow again. This is what can happen in your home. Move one mass of junk out of the way, and all the energy that had been trapped in that pile is suddenly available to help you move your vision forward.

But how do you get started? Which log do you move first? Surprisingly, the first step has nothing to do with actually cleaning. You don't need to put a single thing away yet. Rather, the first step is to make a quantum shift in the way you view yourself. In essence, your surroundings are an expression of your inner self, and they profoundly impact your outer self. If your environment is failing you in some way, perhaps you are failing yourself. What is it that is keeping you from having the home that you want? What is it that is missing in your life? Why are you holding onto items from your past that no longer serve a purpose in your life? Do you feel in some way unworthy of an attractive home? Guilt is commonly associated with material possessions. Shame about having either too much or not enough leads many people to hide behind piles of stuff. Just as an overweight person may eat to "hide" his or her true self, messy people may have constructed a moat of stuff around them that says, "Keep out!" Our possessions can serve as extremely effective shields against the outside world. It is no surprise that a cluttered existence is considered a symptom of depression.

Sometimes shopping is the path to disorder. We live in a society that espouses shopping as a legitimate path to happiness. As a culture, we celebrate excess. Unhappy people tell themselves that they just need five more pairs of shoes or another set of power tools to feel better, Shopping can provide a momentary high, but the trip is short-lived. Soon enough those Costco bags have overrun the pantry and are spilling out into the kitchen. Shopping that starts as a solution quickly becomes a problem. As Deepak Chopra writes in *The Seven Laws of Spiritual Success*, "We have traded our self for the symbols of our self." How true!

For others, the mess and clutter bubbles up from a completely different mind-set. These folks don't want to spend money on themselves. They don't feel justified using hard-earned dollars to recover old sofas or buy bookcases. For a variety of reasons, on a subconscious level they feel unworthy of a beautiful, functional space. They think, Why spend money on myself when there is the children's college education to pay for and a retirement to fund? So they hold onto all the possessions they already have, even if they no longer serve any purpose other than to take up space.

As I've stated before, your environment shapes your inner self and vice versa. Uncluttering your home brings instant mental clarity, increases your productivity, and dramatically improves your self-esteem. In fact, you need a living environment that supports you in order to reach your full potential.

I have a client who hadn't bought any new outfits in years. Her clothes were strewn haphazardly throughout her house, and not surprisingly, she could never manage to find the right thing to wear when she was going out. Finally, she built a long-overdue walk-in closet. With a new place to properly store a wardrobe, she was inspired to ditch the old sweatpants in favor of more professional garb. She donated everything that was the wrong size or out of fashion and bought a few new skirts and a couple of dresses. She felt "professional" again for the first time in decades. She began to believe that she could get back in the work force, and she soon found a job to go with the new clothes! Redoing your space can be the impetus for tremendous positive change in your life.

You don't need to spend a fortune to get a beautiful and functional space regardless of your style. This is why we have Ikea, Target, and e-Bay! We are fortunate to live in a design-saturated era. There are dozens of television shows and magazines to supply ideas if you face designing on a budget.

Some people get overwhelmed by their visions. They picture custom-made sofas and crystal chandeliers and are determined not to buy an end table or a light fixture until they find the perfect one. This can go on for years. In the meantime, they are trying to read in the bedroom using the glow from the hall light! I urge readers who are missing a key item in their home—an area rug, a wastepaper basket, a bedside lamp, whatever it may be—to just go get it. Don't compromise your ability to function in the pursuit of perfection. If you find the perfect thing later on, you can always replace the "placeholder" you have in its spot.

On the surface, it seems that having an organized, well-functioning home should be simple. It can be extremely frustrating to see the potential of your space shimmering always just beyond your reach. The fact is that getting and staying organized is not so simple for many of us. You might be completely unaware of the roadblocks you've put in your path to sabotage your success.

If you are about to undertake a major upgrade of your space, set aside a chunk of "quiet time" before you begin to make major changes. Honestly consider your habits and what is at the root of your negative patterns. Awareness is the first step in overcoming your self-imposed obstacles. Lifelong habits don't change overnight, but the steps that I am outlining for you will get you moving forward on the path to quantum change.

Perhaps the most important first step you can take is to forgive yourself for your current mess. Rather than beating yourself up, concentrate instead on how your ideal space would look, and imagine yourself already living in it. Remember that thinking is actually an act of creation and that our thoughts are powerful agents of change. For the moment, don't see yourself as disorganized. Instead of dwelling in negativity, take the eagle view. Living as if the positive changes have already taken place is the fastest way to create positive change in the first place. I'm not saying, though, that books are going to shelve themselves. We'll return to mouse view shortly, get out the sharpies and garbage bags, and go to work. But there is vital inner work to be done first.

Don't rush yourself through the critical first step of visualizing your finished room. Take all the time you need to consciously create an image of your ideal environment. If you are comfortable meditating, it's a great way to get centered before you begin. The third sidebar, below, helps beginners who want to give this powerful tool a try. You may feel a little uncomfortable or kooky doing this exercise, but I encourage you to persevere because it will speed up the whole process. The more intensely you are able to concentrate on your vision, the stronger it becomes. The law of attraction tells us that thoughts really do become manifest. Your vision of your ideal, perfect space should be so real that you can access it through all your senses. If you like candles and flowers in your rooms, you should be able to smell them. You should know how the bedspread feels, what color the throw pillows are, what kind of music is playing in the background.

First, picture the space completely empty. Interior designers like to start with a blank canvas so that they don't get distracted by what currently fills the space. Take a page from their book. Start with a blank slate, and ask yourself what sort of an emotional reaction the space elicits. If it is a restful area, such as a bedroom, what do you want to put in here to help you relax? If it is a workspace, how can you energize the room? Concentrate on the flat surfaces in your room that tend to collect items. Close your eyes and picture the countertops or tabletops in your perfect room. Are they completely clear? If you use a phone in this room, where is it? Does it have a notepad and pen nearby? Envision all the pieces of furniture. They may be pieces that you already own or things that you hope to buy in the future. It isn't necessary to have everything on hand before you start. Allow yourself to dream big. Go ahead and put the flat-screen TV and the granite counters into your vision if they're part of your dream. Everyone will have a unique vision of his or her perfect space. Move carefully through each space in the room, and make all the areas equally "real." It may take you minutes, or it may take days. Allow yourself the time you need to get it right. As the Spanish like to say, "Life is long." There's no need to race through this process. In fact, rushing will compromise your chances of success.

Next, put yourself in the picture. When you are sitting in your reading chair, are your glasses nearby? If you are in the family room, are all the remotes within easy reach? Imagine yourself doing a variety of tasks. This takes some thinking for rooms like the kitchen. If you are at the sink doing dishes, do you have a sponge, gloves, and dish soap all at hand? Consider the equipment you'll need to cook various dishes. Is the bread maker handy? Can you reach the pots? Can you make coffee without clearing a space first? It's fine to take a moment to role-play in your space, picturing different possible places for your cups and spoons, but resist the urge to actually start moving things around for now.

When your vision of your space is really complete—you can appreciate it with all five senses and you've pondered the various uses—go ahead and open your eyes. Don't let those great ideas get away from you! Feel free to grab a pen or run to the computer and record your results. It can be helpful to get ideas from magazines for inspiration. Tear out these pages and file them in separate binder pockets or folders, one for each area you'll be organizing. Better yet, construct an inspiration board and hang it where you can see it every morning. This will serve as a reminder to make fixing up your space a priority. I am also a strong believer in lists. Keeping lists as you progress through your vision is another great way to support your goals. Ideas are always more powerful once they are written down. You can repeat the process of visualizing your space as often as you like. In fact, the more time you spend hanging out in your imaginary room, the easier it will be for you to make it real.

By using all the tools at your disposal and envisioning your space from many different perspectives, you are clarifying the changes needed and giving yourself the gift of your unique vision. Once you see what your space could be, you will be much more driven to start the work of creating your ideal room. In the process, by focusing on the future, you also can begin to forgive yourself for past mistakes. This is a vital step in moving forward. Congratulations, you are on your way!

Clarifying Your Vision: Questions to Ask Yourself

Use these questions as a guide when creating your vision:

- How do you use this space? List all the things you do here.
- What is currently working well in this area?
- What doesn't work? How can you improve this?
- How do you feel in this space right now?
- How do you want to feel in this space once it is organized and meets your needs?
- What is in this room that is not needed here?
- What is missing from this room that should be added?
- Does everything you use in this room have a place to be stored?
- What color and style is the finished room? (Modern, spare, and neutral or shabby chic and cozy?)

Cozy Nooks Every Home Needs

There is an endless variety of uses for any one room, and it is fascinating to me to see how different people live. I have seen dining rooms used as bedrooms, garages turned into offices, and desks made from doors, to name just a few. However, regardless of whether you are living in a midcentury modern ranch or an antique colonial, certain functions are common to all homes. As you read through this list, ask yourself if you need to create one of the following spaces in your home:

- A quiet, private spot for reading, journaling, or meditating (there should be a nook that is just right for each member of the household)
- A place to gather for conversation
- A place to have meals
- A dedicated space for working
- A peaceful place for sleeping
- An organized spot to do laundry
- A clutter-free spot for washing dishes and preparing food
- Special nooks for children with the items they need
- Special nooks for pets with the items they need
- A storage space for bulky items not currently in use (winter comforters, for example)

- A "launch pad" for coats, boots, shoes, backpacks, cell phones, and whatever else you use in transit to and from your house
- A permanent location for your keys and wallet or handbag (this ensures that you'll never again be late because you couldn't find your keys or wallet)

Some professional interior designers and architects do "test runs" in rooms before building them. They place masking tape on the floor to mark the future positions of walls, furniture, and appliances. Then they ask their clients to pretend to unload groceries or cook dinner in the marked-out kitchen. After you have a clear vision of your space, you can try this same technique. It can be ideal if you are ordering furniture on-line and want to check out the scale of the piece of furniture in your actual room.

Meditation for Beginners

Meditation is a way of quieting your mind so that you can be more peaceful and focused. It plays a role in many religions, but meditation need not have any religious component. Here is how to do a basic meditation:

Sit in a comfortable position. As long as your spine remains straight, you can sit in any posture you like, including in a chair. Close your eyes, and concentrate on the darkness behind your eyelids. Let your thoughts flow, but do not focus on any particular idea. To keep your attention focused, you can chant a simple mantra, such as "Om" or any other word or syllable, or focus on your breathing. If you get distracted and start to think, just return to concentrating on your breath or your mantra. After about ten minutes, open your eyes. Try to do this at least twice a day, slowly building up to twenty minutes at a time. With practice, you will find your mind clearer, and you will feel more content and better able to concentrate. Your decision-making abilities also will improve. Many scientific studies have shown that meditation relieves stress.

If you have trouble sitting, try active meditation. You can walk while meditating. Concentrate on each step that you take, trying to make each one as smooth as possible. These techniques take practice, but with time, the rewards are well worth the effort.

I believe that meditation, although not directly linked to organizing your home, definitely will aid you in the process. You may have many passing thoughts about your space during a meditation that will help you focus when you become active again. It is also a fantastic way to relax. After all, change is always a little stressful.

What to Keep, What to Let Go

In the next chapter we will go through your entire space and review what you need versus what you can afford to heave. However, a little preview at this point may help you to visualize your ideal space. Don't forget—items that clutter drain energy. Don't feel obligated to hold onto anything. If that rare but chipped teacup from your aunt leaves you cold, don't hesitate to give it the heave-ho. However, if you have a collection that you value, there's no reason to relegate it to a dark closet. I collect cookbooks. I don't use them all that often, but seeing them gives me pleasure, so I have shelved them in my living room. Ditto for my southwestern kachina dolls, which are happy reminders of my travels. For me, the room would feel empty without these items, even though they are mostly decorative. Feel free to make the same choices about your belongings. But also remember that opening up a previously cluttered spot allows new energy and new ideas a place within which to grow.

Feng Shui the Fast Way

Feng Shui is the ancient Chinese art of arranging space in harmony with the environment. Good Feng Shui is believed to promote health, prosperity, creativity, positive relationships, and self-confidence. The practice of Feng Shui is very site-specific. Its many complexities are too intricate to be included in all their depth here. If you are interested, I urge you to browse through some of the many fine books available on Feng Shui. Here are a few simple Feng Shui tips that you can apply to any space without further study:

- Mirrors help move *chi* through your home. Mirrors without sharp corners are especially useful. Make sure you can see your full head in the mirror. Hanging a mirror too high or too low can cut *chi*. A popular spot for mirrors is behind the stove! A double reflection of the stove and burners is said to bring prosperity.

- Use live plants in your home. Live plants create positive energy, but dead plants drain energy, so if you can't maintain houseplants, you are better off not having them.

- Don't keep clutter under your bed. It blocks the energy of the people closest to you.

- In Feng Shui, the state of your kitchen reflects the state of your health, particularly your liver, which detoxifies your body. An organized kitchen can lead to a healthier, less toxic lifestyle.

- The entryway to your house is called the "mouth of *chi*," and its appearance determines the quality of the energy that enters your home. It is also where careers and opportunities enter your life. An entryway or foyer is a perfect place for a beautiful piece of art or an important object, but not for clutter, which will prevent positive energy from entering.

- To prevent opportunities from "draining" out of your life, keep bathroom doors and toilet lids closed. A dripping faucet is believed to symbolize wasting money. Open toilet lids in master baths are said to weaken your sex drive!

CHAPTER 3

Assessing Your Space

And the day came when the risk it took to remain tight inside the bud was more painful than the risk it took to blossom.

—Anais Nin

When one door of happiness closes, another opens; but often we look so long at the closed door that we do not see the one which has been opened for us.

—Helen Keller

Have you every noticed how once you clean and organize a space, suddenly it's the most popular spot in the house? I have seen this many times myself. When I clear the magazines off the coffee table in the family room, it suddenly becomes a magnet for my guests. My daughter sees the newly cleaned family room and brings her book in there to read, curling up under the afghan on the couch. The space looks so inviting that you just feel like you have to spend a few spare moments in the room. There is no mystery in this, of course. People are drawn to the freely circulating energy that imbues a neat, attractive, and well-ordered space.

The opposite is equally true. When my dining room table is overflowing with bank statements and bills, the idea of hosting a dinner party is overwhelming. Before I extend the invitations, I am running through my mental checklist of all the tasks I need to complete before I can even start cooking: Sort and file all those papers, dust the table, find the china and linens (who knows where they are!), iron the tablecloth and napkins (why didn't I do that before I put them away?), hunt around for the recipes

I can never find when I need them, and so on. Pretty soon that dinner party doesn't sound like such a great idea.

Sound familiar? When you live with disorder, you deny yourself countless positive opportunities. If you start every day with a mountain of things that need to be put in order before you get to the important work at hand, you will never reach your full potential. My hope is that *Quantum Organizing* will help you to get out of that rut. When your space is in order, you can get right down to the task at hand, whether it is filing your taxes, sending out your Christmas cards, or just watching a movie. Our lives are already so hectic and complicated, why allow additional obstacles to block our path?

In this chapter I will discuss simple steps to follow to remove the physical clutter and psychic noise from your life. Imagine what a pleasure it will be to step into your kitchen in the morning to make your coffee and find clear counter space to sit at and read the paper. When its time to leave the house, your keys, pocket book, briefcase, shoes, and coat will be neatly arranged within arm's reach of the door, and it will take you mere seconds to leave the house. Some of you may already be living this way, but I suspect for many of you these bonuses of an orderly life seem forever out of reach. But I assure you that it is possible to bridge this gap between your reality and your real potential. You can have an orderly life.

Expect some hidden gems and surprises once you start to introduce order. If you've misplaced some special item, you may discover that its been right under your nose all along.

There is a Sufi story about a notorious smuggler. Each day when he crossed the border on his donkey, the border guard conducted a thorough search, rummaging through the smuggler's belongings. The guard never found anything illegal in the saddlebags. Years later, the guard finally asked the fellow what he was smuggling, since he had never been able to find it. The thief replied, "I was smuggling donkeys, of course!"

If you are feeling a little tense about the work ahead, don't be. One of my fundamental principles of organization is that you have to start from a positive place in order to create positive change. We are all about forward momentum here. If you dread the work ahead, you are essentially telling yourself—and the universe—that you want to quit before you even start! There are no rigid deadlines here. A plan of attack can take just a few minutes to formulate, or it can take days. Allow yourself the freedom to explore your space at your own pace. Don't let yourself become overly emotional. Now is emphatically not the time to berate yourself for falling short of your goals. A detached point of view is best. Before you begin filling boxes, set realistic expectations for yourself. If you have one room to tackle that isn't too hard, start there. It is important to start off with a sense of momentum. If you are a person who tends to burn out after an hour of cleaning, then plan to spend only one hour. Schedule yourself for success. My mom, who is retired now, worked as a physical therapist with stroke patients. She didn't wait until they could walk a mile to start therapy. At first, she expected just one step from a patient. Maybe the patient would do two steps the next day. She always celebrated her patient's progress, no matter how small the incremental achievement was.

Overcoming bad habits is hard work. Don't hesitate to reward yourself with a glass of wine or a long walk when you meet a goal that you have set. As Confucius said, "A journey of a thousand miles begins with a single step." Most of you will not be able to complete all the steps outlined below in one session. That's fine. As long as you keep putting one foot in front of the other, eventually you will get there.

The first step of assessment in quantum organizing is to look at the big picture. Take an "eagle's view" of the entire space that you want to revamp. Look at the placement of the furniture—is it working? Are there clear paths of entry and exit? Are the chairs comfortable? Do you have enough tables and lamps?

What goes on in this room? Making a list of each of the activities that you do in a space is very useful. Think about how you use the space and how it helps you to accomplish your goals.

Evaluating an area in your home that is already functioning well is one way to start organizing. Can you apply a system that is working for you in your tidy kitchen to your toy-strewn playroom or disastrous linen closet? Now review your vision of the space in its most ideal state. Where are the discrepancies between how you envision the space and how the space currently looks?

Another way to target problem areas is to recognize which spaces seem to embody the most stress for you. How do you feel when you enter that boot-strewn mud room or closet whose shelves are bowed with extra stuff? Every object in your home should support your goals in a tangible way. Although the size 4 jeans from the 1970s may very well come back into style, wouldn't you really rather open up that space in your closet for something new? Keeping items around that no longer have a place in your life drains your energy and prevents new things from entering.

New things can lead you to new ways of thinking; new ways of thinking can create tons of energy and forward momentum. You owe it to yourself to make the effort to evolve.

Don't forget to assess some of your out-of-the-way spots as well. I find some amazing things in my car trunk! Sometimes I stash bags of cat food there because my cat has a tendency to rip the bags open if she discovers them in the house. My garden shed is another treasure trove. Garages, garden sheds, basements, and attics are places that tend toward disorder, although they can provide vital support to the rest of your more lived-in spaces. If storage areas are organized, you living areas will function more smoothly as well.

There is a tipping point in personal organization as well as in business. Once you start to make changes, you will quickly witness a snowball effect. Clear two or three small areas, and the results are so pleasing that you'll want to do more. Once you dive in and have a few small victories, the whole job becomes manageable. So lets go!

Assessing Your Space: A Plan of Attack

Here are the detailed steps to follow to organize your space. An abbreviated "quick start" version of these steps appears in the next chapter.

1. *Do a gap analysis of your space.* In business, companies analyze the "gap" to assess where they are versus where they want to be. You can do the same thing in your home. Take another look at your vision from the last chapter. Now "open your eyes" and see your room as it is. How far away are you from your ideal? What do you need to do to bridge this gap? Take in the big picture, and don't get bogged down in the details yet. Think "I need a clear space on my desk to work" rather than "I have to sort through all two hundred of those papers on my desk so I can work!"

Take action: Write down a few notes about your observations. List the major changes you want to make.

2. *Find an area in your home that is already organized.* If there is a spot in your home that is functioning well, take a minute to appreciate it. Congratulate yourself on this little oasis of order! How does this space make you feel? Can you borrow some of the principles that are working here and apply them to a less successful area? How is it organized? Why is it comfortable for you in this place?

Take action: Find a system or an element from this well-functioning space that is transferable to your new space.

3. *What's in the room that should be discarded altogether?* Let's face it, most of us live with more things than we actually need. One of my clients cleans with a trash bag in hand. She is ruthless and pitches absolutely everything that she can. What is in this space that you really can live without? Do you need two years' worth of *People* magazine? Do you need every mermaid picture your six-year-old draws or just a few of her best?

Take action: Go through the space you are organizing, and eliminate everything that is not needed. Make two piles or use two bags: one for items to throw away and one for items to give away. Place the piles or bags adjacent to each other because you may find that items migrate from one pile to another before you've finished. Once you are done collecting, move these piles out of the space altogether. If there are large pieces, such as furniture, you may need to partition an adjacent room into keep and giveaway spaces. You want the space you are organizing to become as close to a blank slate as possible. This will help you to envision new possibilities for the room. Most designers prefer to work with a "blank canvas" because it is much easier to see the potential of an almost empty space.

What to Keep and What to Purge

Answer these seven questions to know what to keep and what to purge:

1. Does this object support my vision of the space?

2. Does it reflect who I truly am?

3. Do I use it or absolutely love it?

4. Does it have sentimental value? How upset would I be if it were lost or broken?

5. Does it have a place in my home? (Where do I store it?)

6. Does it have a purpose in my life? (Is it useful?)

7. How many times have I used it or worn it in the last two years? (If the answer is less than five, let it go.)

Here are some items you can always target for elimination:

Old papers

Outdated newspapers or magazines

Gifts you never liked

Clothes that don't fit

Spare parts for electronic equipment that you no longer have

Parts you can't identify or remember their origins

Kitchen gadgets that no longer work

Damaged and broken items

Old, dried-out cosmetics

Stained towels, especially dish towels

Old phone books

Dead (and half dead) plants

Many of my friends find it very difficult to discard gifts, even items they vehemently dislike. After all, gifts are expressions of love. The givers may have put a lot of energy into buying something meaningful. But facing unattractive objects that serve no purpose in your life is actually stressful. It is impossible to create a room that feels serene if it is filled with clutter.

Of course, people's clutter barometers are calibrated differently. What one person finds intolerably busy may look like a Zen paradise to someone else. One of my friends adores pigs. In her living room, she chose to display just a few special collectible pigs that were meaningful to her. As friends discovered her hobby, they added to her collection. It didn't take long for her modest cache to grow.

Every holiday and birthday brought new ceramic pigs into her life. Soon her collection started to overwhelm the rest of her space. But how could she box up all these good intentions and shove them off stage? Wouldn't her friends want to see their pig when they came to visit? I had to talk her down off that ledge! After all, friends want to see you happy, and these little piggies were no longer a source of pleasure for her. I explained to her that yes, you absolutely want to honor your friendships, but when your friends come to visit, they want to feel comfortable and welcomed. If your space is packed to the brim with bric-a-brac, no one is going to feel relaxed. By leaving some open space, you create room for the friendships to grow and expand. When your body is boxed in, so is your spirit.

If you have friends who live in tiny city apartments, pay attention to how they consider purchases. For many apartment dwellers, open space is precious. They will rarely bring home something new without first removing something else. They are constantly editing their belongings. This is a good habit for everyone to model.

It isn't necessary to callously discard objects. You can certainly repurpose things in your house—move some pigs to a high open shelf in the kitchen, for example. You also can find new homes for things. It's wonderful to share your passions with others who have the space to enjoy them. All the initial good energy of that gift travels with it to a new home.

4. *What is in the room or space that doesn't belong there?* View your room with fresh eyes. It's easy to become blind to all the junk we accumulate over the years. You may forget that the pile of clothes stashed on the floor of the guest closet really doesn't have a place there.

Take action: Make a list of all the things that need to be moved to a new place. You can use this later to help relocate those items. Now take out all the items that don't belong in the space. If you can't find a new place for something immediately, put it in a central area outside the space you are currently organizing. Feel free to remove additional items at any time. If the items are small, gather all of them into one box. Later you can tote the box from room to room and distribute all the items in one trip.

5. *Create zones.* Go clockwise around the room starting at the entrance, and analyze each area within the space. Some designers refer to these smaller areas as *zones*. A zoned kitchen will have a zone for baking, a zone for washing dishes, a zone for paying bills. Every room has zones, and part of your job is to clearly define the zones for yourself. It is much easier to put away the DVDs if all the television watching stuff is clustered in one spot. Review your list of activities that take place in the space. Does each activity have a zone? Group like items together—such as games with puzzles and spare reading glasses with books.

Take action: Move items into their proper zones. Take note of what furniture or storage pieces you may be missing. Practice using your zones. Do you have what you need in each area?

6. *What is missing?* If you have a reading chair, do you have a table lamp and a spot to put down a drink? Look at your space closely.

Imagine yourself doing different tasks. What's easy to do? Which tasks are not being supported by the space? Refer back to your vision. Keeping in mind all the activities that take place here, make a list of what you need that's missing.

Take action: Remembering your vision, add a few of the missing items that can be found elsewhere in your house or purchased quickly nearby. Make a list of everything else you need to purchase. If it takes time to find the perfect end table, that's okay. Some people will only feel comfortable if the space matches their vision exactly. However, if you are not using the reading chair because you haven't found the perfect lamp yet, you might want to consider using a temporary "placeholder" for now.

7. *What is in the right room but the wrong spot?* Do you have to get out of bed to turn out the lights? Are your children's toys where they can reach them, and can they put them away by themselves? Are flower vases stored near a sink? Think about your zones, and make the best choices possible for storing your items.

Take action: Move misplaced items into their proper zones.

8. *Study the flow of energy in the space.* Does the floor plan work? And what's on the floor? Can you move easily throughout the space? Remember that *chi*, or energy, will stagnate if it can't flow easily around furniture and through doorways. Imagine a stream running through the space. Does the water flow unimpeded from one end of the room to the other? Is the furniture in the room "balanced"? Both sides of the room should have a more or less equal weight. If you have a large sectional sofa or bed on one side of the room, you will want to balance this out with another equally sized grouping opposite it. Consider how you will care for the space. Is the flooring easy to maintain? Can you vacuum or sweep without having to move furniture and planters out of the way? Is the vacuum easily accessible to the room? If you have a messy spot in your room like a birdcage or a plant that needs daily cleaning, it's useful to stash a small hand vacuum nearby. Is there a cozy rug by the bed for bare feet or a doormat outside the exterior door?

Take action: Make sure that traffic can flow easily through the space. Move furniture or other objects if necessary to make the floor plan work for you. Try to create balanced groupings of furniture and art. Store cleaning supplies for the space in a convenient location. You will maintain the space better if your supplies are easy to reach.

9. *Is the lighting appropriate?* Lighting can contribute a great deal to the atmosphere of a room, and it's an easy way to vary the mood of a space. Make sure that you have enough light to read or cook and that you also can dim the lighting for a more romantic or contemplative mood. Dimmers are helpful but not absolutely necessary. Having several lamps in the room gives you the option of turning a few off to create a quieter mood. Decorators often recommend positioning a light in each corner of a room, as well as spotlights to highlight important features such as artwork or a fireplace. Table lamps should be placed near each sitting area if possible.

Take action: Move your lamps around to ensure that there are no dark areas and that you have all the task lighting you need.

10. *Is the space attractive?* Does it feel nurturing to you? Don't underestimate the power of design. You can organize so that every paperclip is precisely aligned, but if the room feels cold and sterile, it will not support you. Have a few things in every room that you find beautiful: flowers, candles, or scents. A small water feature is a wonderful Feng Shui touch that can foster the flow of *chi*. Take the time to coordinate your furnishings and decor, paying special attention to color, pattern, and texture. There is no need to rush out and make everything perfect today, unless that's your style, but do try to coordinate as best you can. Eventually, you will find the perfect night stand, but you won't recognize it if you don't spend some time envisioning what it is you want.

Take action: Make a list of what you need to buy or change to make the space welcoming to you. Poke around the rest of your house. You may be surprised to find that you have in another room the item you need here. Add some decorative touches such as live plants and mirrors to bring positive energy to the space.

11. *Put the space to work.* You're nearly done. Get ready to enjoy your new space, and be sure to reward yourself for a job well done when you finish this last step. The final task is to clean the space so that it will be as close to your initial vision as possible.

Take action: Once you have your room reorganized, clean the whole space top to bottom. Vacuum all upholstery and carpets, dust all the flat surfaces, wipe down the windowsills, and wash the panes. Feel free to break this final step into smaller jobs and spread them out over time if you feel overwhelmed. Once you finish, you will feel the positive power of the law of attraction go to work. You will be amazed at the ease with which you can accomplish tasks in this neatly organized space. Chores that seemed difficult before will seem quite doable now. Congratulate yourself on a job well done, and expect to see more positive changes follow.

12. *Finishing touches.* To make sure that you continue to progress, don't delay too long before tying up any loose ends. Organize your lists in a way that makes sense for you, and make it a point to do one or two items each day so that the room continues to grow closer to your ideal. For example, if you are missing a container for your magazines, make it a point to get one. Don't let the job stay "almost finished" indefinitely. Hold yourself accountable. Continue to focus or meditate on your vision of the space. If you concentrate on what you want and live in the space as though it is already perfect, soon enough it will be!

CHAPTER 4

Quick Start: Quantum Organizing for People in a Hurry

Have nothing in your houses that you do not know to be useful or believe to be beautiful.
—William Morris

Reduce the complexity of life by eliminating the needless wants of life, and the labors of life reduce themselves.
—Edwin Way Teale

If you're the type who likes to skip the fine print, throw away the directions, and dig right in, start here. The most important step in beginning the quantum organizing process is to tackle something rather than waste energy spinning your wheels and feeling overwhelmed. As soon as you organize one messy area, you will start to build the momentum you need to tackle the rest of the job. Claiming an early victory is important. It will give you the confidence you need to persevere throughout the rest of the project. Pick one trouble spot, and do the following steps immediately.

Step One

Set a time limit. Organizing is less overwhelming if you commit to a set time frame. Tell yourself that you will work for half an hour, an hour, or a full day, and stick to it.

41

Step Two

Clear the space as completely as possible. You will want to create a blank slate. Remove *all* items from the area. If the area is large, work on one section of the space at a time. Carry a trash bag and a donation bag with you as you work. This way you will be ready to dump and to donate as soon as you finish the room. Resist the temptation to immediately relocate the stuff that doesn't belong. That will slow you down. Instead, gather all the items to be relocated into a box. When you are done organizing, you can make just one trip through the house and deposit them in the proper spots as you go.

Step Three

After removing everything from the room and into an adjacent area, sort your items into four piles:

1. Keep

2. Give away (or sell)

3. Store somewhere else

4. Trash

Piles can be stored in paper grocery bags for small spots or laid out on blankets or tarps for larger spaces.

Note that these steps must be done in order. Procrastination can have dire consequences. If you leave a pile of giveaways in a bag by the front door for a week or more, you will deny yourself the sense of accomplishment you richly deserve. Resist the temptation to interrupt your work as well. Now is not the time to call friends to tell them what you've found, to skim an old magazine, or to try on an old outfit.

Step Four

Immediately throw away all the trash.

Step Five

Immediately put away as best you can all the items that are supposed to be stored somewhere else.

Step Six

Bag all the items to give away, and put them in your car or by the front door.

Step Seven

Take a hard look at what you have left. See Chapter 2 for a list of what to keep and what to let go. Run each item through this list of recommended questions. For each and every expendable item, do one of three things:

1. Throw it away,

2. Add it to your giveaway pile.

3. Find it a new and better place.

Step Eight

Find a place for everything. Clean the area. Review the items that remain. Is anything missing? Do you need a straw tote bag for your magazines or a box for the screws? Do you have a reading lamp for the table? Make a written list of what your space is missing. If possible, wait to put the area back together until you have gathered the containers and extension cords you need.

Step Nine

Evaluate the flow of the space. Can you walk easily through the room, or do you need to reposition some furniture? Can you reach office supplies while sitting at your desk? Well-organized spaces have everything needed for a task within easy reach.

Step Ten

Put everything back in its new place. Tweak as needed. Now that you have taken the time to organize everything, don't forget to maintain it. Discipline yourself to put every item away when you are finished using it.

Congratulations! Don't forget to take note of how energized the space feels now that it is functioning well. You've generated the momentum required to transform your entire home into a lovely and well-functioning space. According to the law of attraction, order attracts order, so don't be surprised if you feel suddenly inspired to tackle the next area on your list!

The Broken-Window Theory

Just as order attracts order, disorder attracts disorder. Have you ever noticed that once the first item goes astray, it doesn't take long for the entire area to spiral out of control? One of my clients has a window seat in her foyer. Fortunately or unfortunately, it is the perfect spot to stash the mail that is waiting to be sorted. However, as soon as the mail is allowed to rest there in a neat (or not so neat) pile, the law of attraction goes to work, and sure enough, more junk starts to appear. By the end of the day, the mail has been joined by the kid's backpacks, the dog's leash, her husband's bike helmet, and so on. Social scientists have given this phenomenon a name. It's called the *broken-window theory,* referring to the tendency for small areas of disrepair, such as broken windows, to spread. Don't allow that coat to hang on the back of your kitchen chair for more than a minute. If you do, you're likely to find that an entire coat family has joined it the next time you turn around!

Stuff You Can Live Without

Every home is different, but many of us tend to collect the items listed below. These are everyday items that almost everyone can live without:

- Old papers
- Outdated newspapers and magazines
- Gifts you never liked
- Clothes that don't fit
- Parts from electronics you no longer own
- Mysterious spare parts

- Kitchen gadgets that don't work
- Damaged and broken items
- Old, dried-out cosmetics
- Stained towels (especially dish towels)
- Old phone books
- Dead (and half dead) plants

CHAPTER 5

Public Spaces

They . . . threw themselves into the interests of the rest, but each plowed his or her own furrow. Their thoughts, their little passions and hopes and desires, all ran along separate lines. Family life is like this—animated, but collateral.

—Rose Macaulay

Live simply so that others might simply live.

—Gandhi

The trouble with simple living is that, though it can be joyful, rich, and creative, it isn't simple.

—Doris Janzen Longacre

It is wonderful to get to know people better by seeing how they live. We've all experienced the revelations that often come when you see friends or acquaintances in their native habitat, so to speak. You can tell if they are nesters by their comfy sofas and lush houseplants. Another person may be always on the go with nothing in the refrigerator and just the bare essentials in place. Regardless of our personal living styles, most of us want our friends and family to feel comfortable visiting us in our homes. This takes planning. People who live in disorganized homes are often ashamed of the disorder and unable to function effectively. Eventually, they stop inviting people to visit. When a friend offers to stop by, they make excuses. Shutting people out of our lives does more than make us unhappy or disappointed. It actually could make us sick! Positive relationships are essential to our growth and happiness. When we avoid this potent source of positive energy, we can quite literally damage our health and well-being. Of course, there's no great harm in asking your mother-in-law to postpone a visit until after you've put the laundry away. But if you find yourself constantly avoiding giving dinner parties because you can't clear a space to eat at the dining room table, you need to change your ways!

When guests enter our home, their first impressions provide them with a lot of information about us. After a quick tour, visitors to my home can tell that I'm an avid and eclectic reader by the tidy pile of books parked beside my cozy armchair. My mementos from around the world speak to my love of travel, and the missing TV in my living room says that I don't give the television center stage. My furniture is overstuffed, but the rooms are not. I like to entertain in small groups, so my furniture is grouped that way. Guests register this kind of information almost unconsciously. Ask yourself what your home says about you and what secrets it reveals. Your vision of an ideal home might be entirely different from mine, but that is what makes life interesting.

There are a few basic organizational concepts you can apply to ensure that your public space is comfortable for both your immediate family and the friends and family who come to visit. In this chapter I outline a plan of attack to help you tackle the disorder in public spaces such as the dining room, living room, and family room. Regardless of where you start, by the end of this chapter you will have organized rooms that reflect your unique perspective. So let's dig in!

The first step is to review your assessment and vision plan for the space. Take a look at the room in front of you. What furniture needs to stay? Can people walk in and out of the space easily? Next, let's start reorganizing so that both the conversation and the energy in these spaces can flow freely.

Grand Entrances and Clean Exits

One space that is shared in every home, no matter how many people live there, is the front entranceway. It is a shame that so many people come and go through their garages or backyards now and ignore their front entrances. The front door is becoming akin to the formal dining room—an imposing space we rarely use. It's too bad because when we enter our homes from the back or the side, we lose the opportunity for meeting our neighbors. Your front door is the very first thing people see when they come to visit. It is also the portal for *chi* to enter your home. This makes it an especially powerful space. According to the tenets of Feng Shui, if energy is prevented from flowing easily into your home, the people who live inside will feel sluggish and even unbalanced or anxious. Visitors may feel unwelcome. And if the entranceway is poorly planned, Feng Shui has it that opportunities will be hindered from entering, too.

Let's start with the door itself. Does the doorbell work? Are there sconces or lanterns outside the door so that nighttime visitors can find the doorbell? Is there a place for the mail carrier to leave the mail other than in a heap inside the door? Is there a doormat? Details do make a difference to your guests. For example, they'll appreciate it if your house or apartment number is legible and easy to read from a distance.

Now reassess the area around your doorway. If you have a porch, you are lucky! I adore porches. I like to imagine myself sitting on a grand Victorian porch with a glass of lemonade in my hand. Too often porches get ignored. If you own one, consider including a cozy spot to sit and greet neighbors. And try to resist the temptation to use your porch or patio as a storage area. When you allow rakes, hoses, and yard toys to accumulate there, you telegraph to the whole neighborhood that your life lacks order. My guess is that if you're reading this book, "disorganized" is not the impression you want to make. Make a mental note of what you want to remove from your entryway. Personally, I would heave any plastic plants, whether they reside inside or outside your house. I know they require zero maintenance and can look real, but they don't add any energy to your home. Live plants, on the other hand, are loaded with positive *chi*. For my clients who lack a green thumb, I recommend low-maintenance choices such as spider plants or jade plants.

Your front entryway is an excellent backdrop for potted plants or a water feature. Including natural elements such as water, earth, and stone energizes a space and has a calming effect. However, overgrown landscaping blocks the positive flow of energy into and around your home, so it's important to keep up with your yard care.

If the exterior of your home looks to be in good order, step inside. Is the space warm and inviting or dark and cluttered? Your front hall is not the place to heap piles of coats and two weeks of mail. You want this area to be clutter-free. However, this is a great place to display flowers or candles and an important piece of artwork or two. Notice that I wrote *two*, not twenty! The front hall is not the best place to display large collections. You want energy to flow unhindered through this space so that it can reach the interior rooms of the house. Family photos can be a nice way to welcome guests as well, but pick a few favorites and present them well. Covering a huge wall with unflattering photos in mismatched frames is generally not welcoming to guests. Finally, check to see if your front and back doors line up. If they do, is there a door you can close between the two areas? Or can you add a folding screen to block one's view of this direct path? It is considered bad Feng Shui to have front and back doors in direct alignment because energy flows in the front door and goes straight out the back! Instead, you want that positive energy to flow through all the rooms in your house so that you can benefit from it. If your front door opens directly into your living space, this can be a problem as well. Most people prefer to have a transitional area, so you might want to use a screen or divider to create one if your home lacks this feature.

A foyer needs to function well too. Make sure that you have a place to hang coats and hats, store wet boots out of site, and stash mail and magazines. It is best to get into the habit of sorting your mail the day it arrives. Choose a spot to keep bills that is as close as possible to where the mail is delivered. This negates the temptation to make piles on the bottom stair or on the dining room table! Think of the front and back doors to your home as the launching and landing pads for your space. Imagine all the items that come in and go out of your house on a regular basis. Do you get water deliveries? Do you hang out dry cleaning for pickup? Make an action plan for each of these things so that there is a system in place to transport and store items with a minimal amount of fuss.

If your family routinely enters your home through an attached garage, mud room, or kitchen, these areas warrant some quantum organizing as well. Family is the heart of any home, and family members deserve the same warm welcome as special guests. Back entrances should be tidy and well lit. There should be a spot as close to the door as possible for storing all the stuff that migrates from car to kitchen and back again, such as backpacks, briefcases, and soccer balls. Placing frequently used items in easy reach of the most frequently used door often makes life simpler for everyone. Children can benefit from having their own labeled spaces to keep homework and coats. Many newly constructed homes feature fabulous mud rooms with custom-designed cubbies for each member of the family. But you don't need to pay for custom carpentry to create an orderly space like this for yourself. A row of hooks with an inexpensive bench underneath can serve the same purpose.

Revisit your vision plan and assessment for each of your public spaces. Did you remember to make a plan for your home's entrances and exits? If not, now would be a great time to go back and make a plan for these areas. Don't forget to include guests in your plan as well. If you have frequent visitors, make sure that you have a place to store their coats and boots. What will their first impressions be when they enter your home? If you make visiting comfortable for friends and family, the positive energy in your space will grow quickly. The laws of attraction tell us that when you create a positive vibe in your home, positive experiences happen more frequently there.

Grand Entrances and Clean Exits—An Action Plan

When you are reorganizing your home's entrances and exits, here are some guidelines to get you started: You can move out-of-season coats, sports equipment, etc. to a seasonal storage area such as the basement or attic. This will free up valuable space in your coat closet or mud room.

Things to toss or donate:

Worn, torn, or outgrown outerwear

Broken or outgrown sports equipment

Junk mail

Out-of-date catalogues and newspapers

Children's outgrown shoes and boots

Cleaning supplies that you never use

Coats that are out of style or that you never wear

Broken umbrellas

Extra shopping bags (There is no need to stockpile more than a dozen of these at a time.)

Do you have the following?

Outside:

A tidy, well-lit exterior

Well-groomed landscaping

A safe and uncluttered path to the front door, back door, and garage

A functional doorbell or knocker

An overhang to protect you from rain and snow while you fish for keys

A sheltered place for mail and packages to be delivered

Inside:

Sufficient lighting

A place to stash mail

A separate zone for bills

A bench or chair for taking off and putting on shoes

A coat closet, cubbies, or hooks to store outerwear, backpacks, briefcases, sports equipment, etc.

A place for guests' coats, umbrellas, and boots

A place to hang wet things

A place to remove dirty shoes right at the door

A place nearby to store newspapers and magazines that arrive by mail

Something decorative such as a mirror, painting, or flowers to provide a focal point for the space

A clear path to all the adjoining spaces, including the basement, if you access it

Living Rooms Made to Live In

Now that we have your family coming and going with ease, let's focus on the living spaces of your home. Whether you live alone or have a large family or several roommates, you will want a living space that is both a center for conversation and a haven from the outside world. I know my home is my refuge from the corporate world, and I am always happy to come home to this peaceful space. Perhaps your living room is lively with the frequent comings and goings of guests. As I have mentioned many times throughout this book, we are all unique individuals, and that is why no two living rooms ever look exactly alike. Take a moment to go back to "eagle view." Can you easily accomplish all the things you wish to do in the space? You may have already assessed this area, but if not, take a moment to think through your use of this space and determine what is essential and what is essentially clutter. Review your vision plan of the space as well. The more time you spend envisioning the room perfectly designed to support your needs, the more quickly the law of attraction can go to work to provide it. Of course, you don't get to just sit and wait for it to happen. The universe requires your help! But remaining positive as you face the task at hand is always useful and will help you to complete the nitty-gritty work much more quickly and easily.

Many people choose to make their living rooms the most formal space in the house. If you entertain formally on a frequent basis, this could be a great choice. However, if you feel that your living room is more of a "dead" room, serving as a museum for all the objects and furniture that are too precious to use, you may want to reprioritize. I have a friend whose mother is a talented interior designer. When my friend was a child in the 1960s, her living room was the ultimate in period mod and featured an all-white sectional sofa. Children and pets were not allowed to enter the living room for fear of their ruining the upholstery. It was simply too fabulous for the family to actually *use* it. On those rare occasions when her mother beckoned the children in to greet company or celebrate Christmas, my friend felt awkward and unwelcome. The sectional inevitably became dated and was left behind, but the children's memories of exclusion unfortunately have endured. It is somewhat trite but true to say that we make new memories each and every day. It is wise to be mindful of how our living spaces affect our interactions with the people we love.

When you enter your living room, do you feel comfortable and at ease? Or are you on edge? How will your guests and family feel in the space? If your visitors include pets and children, it is perfectly possible to find a tasteful way to make the living room work for them as well. One of my clients placed some old kilim floor pillows in a cozy corner near a window seat. She propped children's books on the bottom shelf of a nearby bookcase, right at their eye level. A tasteful lidded basket on the floor holds washable crayons, some paper, and some small toys. Kids and pets are instinctively drawn to this "made just for them" spot while adults lounge about in the leather club chairs. After all, it can be difficult to have a good conversation when you are being tugged at by a bored toddler. A little forethought by this hostess made entertaining enjoyable, and she didn't have to sacrifice her own good design sense in the process. This is still a very grown-up space.

When you assess your own living room, take into account everyone who might regularly visit, not just the permanent residents of the home. Is your mother always cold when she visits? Add a beautiful throw to your couch. Does your best friend love to garden? A tiny vase of flowers on your end table certainly will cheer her. And, of course, almost everyone enjoys sharing a small plate of cookies or cheese and crackers when they visit.

It is not surprising that many newly constructed homes feature rather small formal living rooms that function more like old-fashioned parlors and cavernous family rooms. Living rooms have been relegated to an afterthought. However, it is possible to make your living room more central to the flow of your home and not a forgotten space. Try including some activities in your living room that will draw you to the room on a regular basis. It may be the ideal location for a quiet nook where you can read or knit, do puzzles, or listen to music. If you entertain, be sure that your seating plan facilitates easy conversation and that you include a table of some kind to hold drinks and snacks. Do you watch television or movies in the living room? If so, don't forget to consider viewing angles when you position the TV. You may want to put the TV in an armoire that can be closed when the TV is not in use.

Living rooms typically feature a focal point. Some homes are blessed with a fireplace or a great set of windows. The focal point of the room also can be the TV if that makes sense for your family. If your crowd gathers around the "electronic hearth" in the evening, you might want to invest in a flat-screen TV that can float over a console table. This is a more refined look that will blend more easily if you also choose to entertain there. However, good Feng Shui practices suggest that you enclose the TV because electronics are believed to emit negative energy.

Try to arrange your seating so that it directs attention to the most prominent feature of the room, accenting it rather than competing with it. The guidelines of Feng Shui advise against placing seating so that your back is facing a door. You want to be able to see people when they enter the room. This makes good practical sense as well. It is unsettling to hear someone enter before you can see them. Circular seating arrangements are especially good because energy can flow freely around the space. Seating that backs up to a wall is considered a plus as well, but placing sofas under windows is not desirable because you don't want to put yourself or your guests directly in the path of the energy flowing from the door to the window. Placing lamps or other light sources in each corner of the room also will help to maximize the space's energy in addition to making the room more attractive. *Chi* avoids dark corners, so to ensure optimal energy flow, provide adequate lighting on all sides. An abundance of lamps also gives you the option of varying the brightness to fit your mood. Mirrors and live plants also attract *chi* to darker areas of the room.

Tabletops are said to signify health. Keeping them clear is believed to promote the good health of your family and guests. Remember, not every surface needs to have something on it!

It's especially important to think about traffic patterns, too, particularly because you may decide to entertain here. If you are including a bar area, can people move easily around it during a large party? Are there enough chairs to accommodate everyone during large gatherings? Can you easily enter and exit the room without having to dodge furniture? When the energy flows easily, conversations will flow just as easily. Ultimately, living rooms are for "living in," and regardless of the size or style of the room, you should feel comfortable and centered there. A little uncluttering and a well-thought-out seating plan can help you make this central room a center of pleasure for you as well.

Things to Toss or Donate or Relocate

Family heirlooms that you dislike or have negative memories attached

Furniture that does not suit the style of the space

Furniture that does not function in the space (too small, too big, too precious, etc.)

Uncomfortable or impractical furniture

Everything you personally find unattractive, even if it was a gift

Dormitory furniture such as cinderblock shelves and ripped couches (Its time to upgrade!)

Knickknacks and all unnecessary clutter (Preserve a few special pieces.)

CD and DVD jewel boxes with no CDs inside

Books and magazines you have already read

Broken electronics and remotes

Do you have the following?

Clear pathways to, from, and around the room

Comfortable seating for several people

A lamp or lamps near several of the chairs for reading and other projects

A focal point

End tables or coffee tables to hold drinks and snacks

Varied light sources—candles, overhead lights, table lamps

A stereo, boom box, or iPod dock

Storage containers for CDs, DVDs, remotes, etc.

Books and magazines (neatly stored)

An afghan or a throw for cool weather

Flowers or plants

Air conditioning, a ceiling fan, or an electric fan for hot weather

Some objects that are personally meaningful to you as well as decorative

Dishing about Dining Rooms

One cannot think well, love well, sleep well, if one has not dined well.
—*Virginia Woolf*

*We should look for someone to eat and drink with before looking for
something to eat and drink.*

—*Epicurus*

While today's formal living rooms often gather dust, the dining room has become the repository for unfinished projects and
residual stuff. Your son's half-finished science report, last month's
bank statements, and last year's holiday cards have taken over the
dining room table while your family crowds around the kitchen
island to eat. All this junk will get unceremoniously packed away
to make room for the next dinner party, but I suspect in many
homes the clearing up happens only just before the holidays hit.

Your dining room may be part of a shared space. Many new
homes opt out of formal dining rooms altogether and instead
incorporate a dining nook into the central living area of the
home. Wherever the dining table is located, there is something
very special about sitting down to share a great dinner at a table
that has been carefully set. On these occasions, sitting together
to break bread around one central table really does feel special
even when the meal is an informal one. Some families eat at the
dining room table on a daily basis, whereas others reserve it for
holidays or special occasions. Either way is equally wonderful.
The important thing is to have an inviting place to sit down and
eat together. The holiday rituals that develop between friends
and family help to strengthen our connections to each other.

But what happens at the dining room table when it is not
being used for eating? This is where many tables get into trouble.

Once the plates have been cleared from the last celebration and the linens removed, the table gets bored. Pretty soon the junk mail stops by. Next, a briefcase appears along with some wrapping paper and an empty coffee cup. Before you know it, it's a party of a different sort. Sound familiar? For many of us, resisting the siren song of a large, empty, flat surface is very, very difficult. It takes all our willpower not to turn that dining table into a gift-wrapping center or a spare workspace. In some homes, space is at such a premium that families have no choice but to multitask in this space. This is as it should be. There is no reason not to make frequent use of every inch of your home. But you need to put systems into place so that disorder doesn't take over permanently. Ideally, your dining room will be free of clutter every day and not just on the days leading up to a party. The older the junk on your table, the more difficult it will be to release the energy trapped inside. A cluttered dining room also can leave your family feeling pressured because disorder breeds stress. The dining room and kitchen play a key role in nourishing your family both physically and spiritually. Allowing clutter to gather there can have very negative consequences.

The flow of energy through the room should be gentle, not too fast or slow. A crystal chandelier centered over the table can help *chi* to flow more easily, as can a mirror if it is placed to reflect a pleasing image. If possible, position the mirror so that it reflects the food on the table. "Doubling your food" like this is said to double your wealth! However, if your table is full of old clutter, a mirror will double the negative effects of this unfortunate state as well. Boxes of old stuff also may keep your family focused on past issues rather than moving forward in life. If you find that your family seems unable to move beyond old hurts, try sharing a meal in a dining room that has been cleared of everything that evokes unpleasant memories. You might find yourself feeling refreshed and more able to move on. Using a tablecloth instead of individual placemats is also believed to bring diners closer.

In most instances, Feng Shui practices recommend leaving some clear space in the center of a room for *chi* to gather, but the dining room is an exception. Here, it's better to center the table in the room, allowing ample space around its periphery for energy to flow. Soothing colors such as yellow, peach, and beige, along with a thick carpet to soften sounds, can help to keep the room tranquil.

Now that I have impressed on you the importance of clearing all the extraneous items from your dining room, I would like to go out on a limb and suggest that you make a point of eating together here at regular intervals in addition to the holidays. Every family's schedule is different, but try to make it a point to sit down together once a month or once a week or even every night and share each other's company in this newly invigorated space. I think you will notice some immediate positive benefits. This setting affords families the perfect opportunity to relate stories about the day and spend time together. You will increase your chances of success even more if you plan out your dining room in such a way that the space is equally welcoming to each member of your family. Make sure that children can sit comfortably at the table. Go ahead and provide booster chairs if need be so that the children in your life can join the grown-ups at the table. These are easily removed later. During dinner parties, include some decorations that are sturdy enough to be explored by even the youngest diners. Make sure that the more senior members of your party are seated so that they can easily hear what everyone else is saying, and provide chairs that are both comfortable and easy to get in and out of. Pay attention to lighting as well. Dimmers are fabulous in dining rooms. You can lower the lights for an intimate meal and raise them when you are entertaining older guests who don't generally see quite as well in dim lighting.

The next day, when the junk mail files back in along with your daughter's violin, meet them at the door and dispatch them directly to their appropriate places! We all know stuff loves to stay where it lands. It takes more energy to remove the mail from the dining room table than to just leave it there. The trick is to not let the clutter enter in the first place or to put a plan in place to remove items from the room as soon as you are done using them, perhaps daily or weekly.

Providing sufficient storage for the linens and tableware that you use in the dining room also will help to keep disorder at bay. There are lots of creative ways to store dishes and such. In my home, I have a combination kitchen/dining area and store my nice dishes in a bookcase. My daughter, who is a photographer and full of creative ideas, is a scavenger who has found much of her furniture on the curb. Her home looks great because she pulls it all together in an organized fashion. So you don't need to spend a fortune to create a beautiful room. If you can afford a gorgeous, high-end sideboard, fine. But don't worry if you are on a budget. Look for unique pieces that really suit you and your space. If your dining room is small, it is fine to store rarely used dishes, serving pieces, and linens in another location. The perfect quantum quotient of belongings will vary from family to family. The key is to keep on hand only what is essential to your family.

An Action Plan for Dining Rooms

Things to toss or donate:

Dishes, silverware, and platters that you never use

Dishes, silverware, and platters that are the wrong style for your home or that don't blend with anything else you use on your table

Pieces of sets—saucers without cups, for example

Dishes that are too chipped or cracked to use

Furniture that does not serve a function in this space

Decorative items that you don't like or need

Gifts that you have never liked or used, including wedding gifts!

Anything too difficult to maintain (If you know that you will never iron that huge linen tablecloth or polish an elaborate silver tea set, you might consider handing those items down to another family member and replacing them with something better suited to your lifestyle.)

Do you have the following?

Lighting that can be dimmed and/or several different sources of light

A place to store placemats, tablecloths, napkins, etc.

A place to store dishes, serving pieces, vases, candle-sticks, etc.

Comfortable seating for a crowd

A place to spread out food being served (A sideboard is ideal, but your table can work too.)

Easy access to the kitchen for serving and clearing

Sufficient bowls, platters, etc. for entertaining

A design scheme (Can you set the table with what you have and be pleased with the result, or is it too hodge-podge for your taste?)

Friendly Family Rooms

If the family were a fruit, it would be an orange, a circle of sections, held together but separable—each segment distinct.
—Letty Cottin Pogrebin

Cooperation is the thorough conviction that nobody can get there unless everybody gets there.
—Virginia Burden

Family rooms are usually the red-hot center of the home, as well as the room where the most multitasking happens. Family rooms often are where the television, stereo, and video games reside. There may be a computer station, books, and crafts too. And in many homes this is where the toy collection lives—the baskets of Legos, action figures, and headless Barbies all tend to find their way here even if it isn't their intended place in the house.

Many family rooms connect directly to the kitchen, forming the "great rooms" that are all the rage right now. There seems little reason to venture beyond the boundaries of this self-contained space where all the essentials are provided. The problem with great rooms is that we demand a lot from them, sometimes too much. The solution here is careful planning. Before you start rearranging your family room, review your assessment for this space and your vision. You should have a clear idea about all the activities that take place in the space. Next, start to map out a mental floor plan that will allow the room to accommodate these different activities, sometimes simultaneously. Feel free to dream big. The more concrete your vision, the more quickly it will become a reality. Take the time to work through all the necessary details. Then, when you are ready, start to reorganize things.

When you have a tentative floor plan in place, invite your family in to "play" in the space. You can actually move your furniture around, or if you are making major changes, you can clear the space entirely and use masking tape on the floor to mark the position of key items. Now double-check your vision against the reality of your reconfigured space. Do you have a unique zone to accommodate each activity? If there is a toy area, is there sufficient space to spread the toys out to play? Is your DVD collection in easy reach of the DVD player? Is there a good reading light by the couch? Can people comfortably share the space while they are engaged in different activities? If a zone doesn't seem to be working, can it be moved to another room? It is difficult to comfortably combine TV watching with computer use and book reading. Its doable, but is it really necessary?

Now go back to "eagle view" and think more deeply about your vision for this room. Of course, everyone wants a highly functional family room, but don't neglect its spiritual significance. The family room is so named because it is meant to bring your family closer. If the room is properly planned out, not only should it help to keep your family life in order, but it also should deepen the family bonds as well. There are some concrete and quite practical things that you can do to facilitate this kind of bonding. For example, including some group activities such as board games and card games is a great idea. Think also about introducing your family to your own hobbies. If you have a knitting basket next to your favorite chair, it won't be long before one of the kids will be asking you for some needles of his or her own. What a lovely way to share your knowledge.

Merely living in a home where books are prevalent has been shown to be a significant influence on a child's ability to read. Recent studies on literacy have shown that young children who have books in their homes and see parents reading score higher on reading tests, regardless of how much time they actually spend reading themselves. I am not suggesting that you read to your children less! But it's an excellent example of how profoundly our home environment can impact our lives and the lives of our children.

As I've mentioned, both quantum physics and Feng Shui teach us that objects have an energy all their own. The cumulative energy in your environment is constantly influencing you, and in fact, it becomes a part of you. When your shared space is balanced and orderly, your family benefits from the increased positive energy. There are small changes you can make to a family room to increase its *chi* so that it can support your family even better. Here are a few Feng Shui tips: Plants counteract the negative energy emitted by electronics, and they are a wonderful source of positive energy. Light- or medium-green hues are particularly good choices for family room walls because they promote family and health. High-backed chairs and sofas support your family, and family photos should hang on the eastern wall of your room to ensure the good health and well-being of those pictured. Seating arrangements are most beneficial when they face south or east. As in your other rooms, you'll want to make sure that *chi* can flow through the space unimpeded.

Attracting Harmony to Your Family

Sticks in a bundle are unbreakable.
—*Kenyan Proverb*

Coming together is a beginning. Keeping together is progress. Working together is success.
—*Henry Ford*

Once your room is reorganized to maximize the potential of the space, it is time to maximize the potential of your family. The law of attraction can be a powerful tool for families. By concentrating on your shared goals and staying positive as a group, you strengthen the health and well-being of each family member. One of the best ways to accomplish this is to have regular family meetings. Have family members bring a list of what they would like more of in their lives. Agree on one goal that your family will work toward as a group. Next, lay out the concrete steps you need to take together to achieve it.

Goal setting is a wonderful activity for children. It makes concrete the very simple idea that if you want to achieve something, you have to work purposefully toward your desire. This sort of old-fashioned Puritan work ethic is absent in many modern families today. Shuttled from school to soccer to scouts and helped each night with their homework, our children don't get much of a chance to take personal responsibility for their own well-being. It's common for kids to measure their happiness by external standards: Is their bike as cool as their friend's? Is their house as big as their cousin's? There is wisdom in teaching children some responsibility for their own happiness. Does your son want a great bike like his friend? Have him tell the family what steps he'll take to get it.

It is important that everyone agree to work on one family goal at a time. Maybe the backyard needs a basketball hoop, or everyone would like to spend a weekend skiing this winter. Allow each family member to contribute to the process. If your family decides to save money for a vacation, even small children can help by doing simple things such as not letting water run unnecessarily, recycling soda cans, or forgoing that new toy or outfit. You can reduce the grocery bills by agreeing to eat more economical meals for a few months. It can be helpful to fill a change jar with the money you save on the water bill or make a chart to show your progress. Strengthening your family's vision of the goal is an important step toward achieving it. Hanging up an image of your goal, especially one that the kids have drawn, will prove inspiring and move you toward your goal more quickly. It is also important to break the goal down into small, concrete steps. No one should be frustrated by the process. Once you have achieved your first goal, you can start on another one, such as uncluttering part of your house!

Working together as a unit is not common in our current culture. Our society is obsessed with individual goals. If your family is dealing with negativity and dissension, with every member pushing for his or her own wants, putting the law of attraction to work for the group can be a great healing experience.

The law of attraction requires that we remain positive in order for positive change to occur. If your family is focused on bickering and fighting, then it is certain there will be more of it. Creating a tangible prize (a skiing weekend) for staying positive is a great incentive to get your crowd working more purposefully toward positive change.

As a family starts to make progress toward a goal, new behaviors will be further reinforced as good things start to happen. Having a calm and orderly space to work in will further support your family's growth and increase the pace of positive change. As the negative energy in your shared spaces drops, everyone also will start to relax a bit more. Now that you understand how life changing an orderly environment can be for your family, do you really want to let some meaningless junk piled in the toy closet impede your progress? I have given you the incentive you need to finally make your vision a reality so that you can start to see many tangible benefits unfold for the people you love.

A Note on the "Electronic Hearth" (the "Boob Tube")

Family rooms are the primary place we go to relax and decompress from our hectic lives outside the home. Although watching television is much maligned these days, I think there is no harm in a family sitting down and watching a show together once in awhile. Lots of families find watching the Discovery Channel, Animal Planet, or the History Channel a fun way to share their own ideas about important topics. Experts recommend that parents routinely watch television with younger viewers in order to monitor the messages they absorb. (Television is not recommended at all for children under the age of two.) It also allows you to teach your children from an early age to be skeptical of what they see on television, particularly when it comes to advertising. Young children who understand that the purpose of advertising is to convince people to buy products may be less influenced by what they see on television as teenagers. If your family has a Friday movie night, by all means continue this tradition, and set up your family room to support it. Since Feng Shui practitioners believe that electronics can emit negative energy, you might consider enclosing your TV in an armoire so that the doors can be closed when the TV is not in use.

Things to toss or donate:

Toys or games that are broken or missing pieces

Broken or out-of-date electronics

Any item not actually used in the family room

Worn or torn pillows and upholstery

Knickknacks that don't add to the decor or have personal meaning for the family

Photos of any family members who have a negative influence on the rest of the group

Craft projects, puzzles, and games that you have not picked up in over a year

Old photos not worth saving (Try sorting through the boxes, keeping only the very best, and putting them in albums or photo boxes.)

Uncomfortable furniture

Furniture that doesn't function in the space

Do you have the following?

Storage, storage, and more storage!

Proper task lighting for reading and projects, as well as ambient lighting for the room

Clear pathways into and out of the room

A clear space in the center of the room

A blanket, throw, space heater, or fireplace for cold days

A fan or air conditioner for hot days

A seating plan to facilitate easy conversation

Comfortable seating for watching TV or movies if you use the family room for this purpose

Games, puzzles, or other activities that the family can enjoy together

Pets on the Chaise and Playdoh in the Dining Room: How to Make a Place for Everyone and Still Keep Everything in Its Place

The best way to ensure that your family room functions optimally is to create zones for each activity that takes place within the room. Family rooms are used in a lot of different ways. Your zones will not necessarily be the same as someone else's. Some typical zones include entertainment zones, office zones, craft and project zones, reading zones, toy zones, and pet zones. Review your assessment and vision for your family room, and then locate a spot in the room to accommodate each of these zones. Next, use a laundry basket or a box to relocate items to their designated areas. Once everything is in its proper place, be sure you have the proper storage for each item. Do you have a handy place to keep remotes near the television? How about a place for your extra reading glasses near your reading chair? If you like to keep a bottle of water at hand, you will want to have a table on which to set it. If you make sure that everything you need has its place, you'll never again have to burrow between the couch cushions to find the remote.

Storage Options

One thing most living spaces need is plenty of storage. The good news is that today there are lots of stylish options. Even if you are on a budget, you needn't be stuck with primary-colored plastic cubes or cinder blocks with planks across the top. Stores today are stocked with stylish and affordable solutions. Many of the items already in your home can be repurposed. For example, in my home, I store my dining room linens in an antique oak ice box. It's the perfect size. In another area I have an apothecary chest that I use to store CDs. Its drawers and shelves are just right for my collection.

Dual-purpose furniture also can help you to use your living space more efficiently. You can find ottomans with a hidden compartment for storing magazines or an afghan. Small benches that nestle perfectly under a window often come with cubbies underneath that are perfect for holding baskets of toys. Other pieces are designed to tuck into corners, making otherwise unusable space functional. If you can't find a spot for your home office, a corner desk is a tidy solution. When planning storage, don't neglect to make use of your vertical space. Extratall bookcases can be a big help if you have a large library or a collection to display. A small stepladder tucked into a nearby closet can help you to access the upper shelves when you need to retrieve something, but be sure to place more frequently used items within reach.

Teaching Children to Be Organized

It is challenging enough to break your own bad habits and discipline yourself to keep a newly organized room in order. But when there are children in the house as well, the chore of keeping things neat can seem endless. Every day brings a new pile of papers and drawings from school, a precious collection of rocks or bottle caps, and a fresh pile of laundry left in a heap on the floor. That's just for starters. While it is time-consuming to pick up after infants and toddlers, it can seem nearly impossible to keep up with the mess generated by school-age children who can create a path of clutter that extends the length of the house. The fact is, even with the best supermom or superdad intentions, you will fail to have an orderly house if you don't get your children on board with the quantum system. Fortunately, children are much more open to new ideas than grown-ups. When you explain that clutter drains energy from the family, they probably will be less likely to question you than an adult might be. You also can remind them that it is easier it is for them to find homework and lunchboxes in their classroom where everything has a neatly labeled spot. Enlist their help to make things just as simple at home.

If you have younger children, keeping them vested in the process is the key to success. This is their home as well as yours, and you will want them to feel just as energized by your newly organized space. Get their advice on containers and furniture placement, and try to incorporate their suggestions as much as possible. It may not work, though, to have them assist you with your initial reordering of the space. If the area is messy, it can be too overwhelming for young children to help reorganize a large number of toys and books. However, once the space is properly arranged for them, it should be very easy for them to maintain it in the future. And that is the ultimate goal.

Your next step is to create a system for cleaning up that is geared to your child's ability level—and to stick with it. Remember that for toddlers, out of sight is out of mind. They have not yet developed the mental capacity to understand that an object still exists despite its being hidden. For this age group, it is best to store toys in open shelves and baskets that leave the contents visible. Make sure that your children's belongings are stored in places that are easily and safely accessible to them. Children's books and toys should be shelved where they can be reached easily. Preschoolers who are starting to dress themselves do well with low hooks to hang their coats and a place below to stash their shoes or boots, just like they have at school. A clever way to label toys or zones for nonreaders is to use your camera to make a luggage tag. Take a photo of the item to be stored in the container, and then tape it or tie it to the storage container itself.

Once the room is finally in order, it is time to explain to your children how the space is meant to function. If the drawing supplies are all in one basket, and the basket is meant to be stashed in the arts and crafts zone of the room, you need to spell all this out for your children. When your space is ready to be used, do a walk-through with the whole family, pointing out each zone and what should be stored there. If family members have had a role in creating the space, much of the new system will already be familiar to them. Mimicking organizing systems that children have learned at school can speed up the learning curve at home.

Next, choose a time once or twice a day when you ask the children to help you return toys to their places. Make it the same time each day, and don't vary it unless it is an emergency. You should expect some resistance at first if you have not been routinely asking children to assist with cleanup. It may take a little time, so be patient! But also be persistent. Structure and routine are essential elements here. If you let things slide for a day or two, you will quickly amass a pile that that will overwhelm you both. Should you find that your set pickup time is not sufficient to corral the mess, you might want to consider establishing a one-toy-at-a-time rule. Montessori schools are expert at teaching children to be self-reliant. Montessori classrooms require children to put away one toy completely before they can choose another.

Freely praise and encourage your children throughout this process, but avoid the temptation to do the work for them. Some families find it useful to keep a chart listing chores that can be checked off or marked with gold stickers, whereas other families find this tactic off-putting. Choose what works for you, whether it is handing out stickers or sitting together to read a "reward" book when you are through picking up. Teaching your child to care for his or her things also teaches him or her to care for himself or herself. This is a wonderful gift to give your child and an essential skill to impart. It won't take long for your family to notice how much more fun it is to have a room that's easy to play in and easy to pick up. Give family members the chance to soak up this positive experience, and they will naturally want to maintain it.

CHAPTER 6

Private Spaces

I would rather sit on a pumpkin and have it all to myself, than be crowded on a velvet cushion.

—Henry David Thoreau

Everything should be made as simple as possible, but not simpler.

—Albert Einstein

What a commentary on civilization, when being alone is being suspect; when one has to apologize for it, make excuses, hide the fact that one practices it—like a secret vice.

—Anne Morrow Lindbergh

Everyone needs a quiet place at home where he or she can go to rejuvenate, and for many people, these very private spaces have an almost sacred aspect. It is not uncommon to find a small shrine tucked into a quiet corner of a den or a bedroom or a special spot specifically reserved for meditation. Others recharge by reading in a favorite chair or watching birds at the feeder. Life is so hectic that it helps to have a tranquil spot to reconnect with the big issues in one's life.

Regardless of your spiritual orientation, a chance to be alone with your thoughts is a key underpinning of an organized life. If you lack a home sanctuary of some sort, you may want to ask yourself why. It may be that you are not giving your own need for reflection the weight that it deserves.

To go on a vision quest is to go into the presence of the Great Mystery.

—Lakota proverb

The Native-American culture recognizes the value of time alone as an integral aspect of self-renewal. In many tribes, adolescent boys mark the passage into adulthood by seeking their spiritual guides through vision quests. The boys spend up to four days in the woods seated in a ceremonial circle, without food or other comfort. Ultimately, each boy encounters an entity who will serve as the boy's lifelong spiritual guide. Although the vision quest most commonly serves as a rite of passage, the Lakota tribe does not limit quests to adolescent boys. Women and men of all ages can undertake a vision quest. During a quest, participants also fill their medicine bags with small tokens, such as feathers or rocks, believed to be sent by their spiritual guides as reminders of their visions. Today our "tokens" may take the form of paperweights, stamps, or old photographs rather than rocks and feathers, but the purpose of "sacred" objects endures. Placing objects that are personally meaningful to you in your private space can be very powerful spiritual "medicine."

Ancient rites of spiritual fulfillment cross cultural boundaries and have wide-reaching significance. Time alone to rethink and rejuvenate is essential for people who hope to continue growing and renewing their spiritual self. Taking a few hours, or even a few minutes, to quietly consider changes in your life is essential. By creating a space to celebrate your own unique desires, you accelerate the process of transformation and bring yourself one step closer to manifesting your highest goals.

Unfortunately, there is a tendency today to devalue the importance of solitude. Being alone is too often confused with being lonely. Surprisingly, the word *alone*, coined in medieval times, did not originally mean "in the absence of others." Initially, it was defined as "a completeness within one's singular being." *Soli-*

tude was used initially to describe "an experience of oneness with God." Our times call for a return to this original definition that so beautifully expresses the positive aspect of private time.

Some people choose meditation as a way to practice being alone, whereas others may write poetry, read a book, or just sit quietly with their thoughts. Regardless of how you choose to spend your private time, there are many quantifiable benefits to be gained. Your subconscious requires alone time to process experiences and unravel problems. If your private space is soothing and beautiful to you, as well as organized, the time you spend there will be even more productive. If your private spaces are not up to snuff, it's possible that your private life is also in disarray.

In some homes, the public spaces are nicely arranged, but the private spaces are a mess. The living room looks terrific. But when you open the door to the master bedroom, you are greeted by an unmade bed and heaps of laundry. The dining room table gleams, but the home office is piled with year-old newspapers and bills. If your home fits this pattern, the source of the problem may lie beyond the clutter. Could it be that on some level you don't think that you deserve the same degree of order and happiness that you provide for others? Is there something in your space or in your life that is holding you back? Creating a beautifully appointed private space is one of the simplest and best ways you can support yourself.

For some people, their private space is their bedroom; for others, it is a small nook or even their garden. Depending on your lifestyle, you may find that you need more than one "quiet room." Perhaps you have a corner in your home office designated for making vacation plans or a spot in your bedroom reserved for reading. Creating these zones for yourself frees you up to focus on what really matters to you and provides a buffer against the hubbub in the rest of the house. Children and spouses need their own spots too—a window seat in a child's bedroom or a big leather chair in a quiet corner go a long way toward restoring family harmony.

Experts agree that "down time" is as essential to children's intellectual growth as it is to adults' well-being. Recent statistics show that in the past twenty years, children's unstructured activities have declined by more than 50 percent while structured sports time has doubled. Today's children cope with many of the same modern pressures that adults do and spend their days in the midst of a crowd at day care, school, and organized activities. A morning perched in a tree trunk or reading a comic book on their bed is rare for most kids. As a child, I did some of my best problem solving during long car rides. Now even this little bubble of privacy has been invaded by DVD players, iPods, and BlackBerries.

When you plan private space in your home, don't forget to address your children's need for private time. You also might create ways for the family to be alone together away from outside interruptions. When it's pizza night, do everyone a favor and leave the BlackBerry, cell phones, and game players turned off. The only people you should be talking to are the ones sitting in the room with you. After all, aren't they the people that matter most?

An Action Plan for Creating a "Room of One's Own"

Review the vision you have created for your private space, whether this is a bedroom, a study, or a cozy nook elsewhere in the house. Make sure that you are supporting all the different activities that take place in this space. Perhaps more so than any other room in your house, your private spaces need to appeal to all your senses. Sometimes these rooms are the most fun to decorate because you can focus on what pleases you without concern for its impact on others. Do you love lavender and flowery chintz? If your partner doesn't share your enthusiasm for these romantic touches, you may not want to use them in your shared bedroom. But if you have a spot that is yours alone, here is your chance to express yourself without having to be concerned about others' reactions.

Now that you are ready to reorganize, check your vision plan against your actual room. Have you removed all unnecessary objects? Does every object have its place? Remember the importance of flow. Walk in and out of the space. Is anything impeding your movement? If so, adjust your floor plan.

Don't forget that rooms have smells as well; some scented candles or room spray can be a lovely touch. Scents help you to center yourself when you are in the space. Humans have an amazing capacity to remember scents as well. Smells evoke memories and associations for us and can act as positive triggers if we let them. The ritual use of a scent such as vanilla (or any scent you like) can become a tool for you. It becomes your brain's cue to relax and focus inward. This is why many stores are experimenting with aromatherapy. Research has shown that people can be very influenced by scent, and in some stores, sales increased dramatically once a pleasing scent was infused into the space. Studies with brain wave frequency have shown that smelling lavender increases alpha waves in the back of the head, which are associated with relaxation. Fragrance of jasmine increases beta waves in the front of the head, which are associated with a more alert state. Aromatherapy has been in use since Roman times over six thousand years ago. Essential oils such as chamomile, rosemary, and lavender can add just the right relaxing note to your space. Just remember not to overdo!

As you begin to create your own little sanctuary, don't forget to select the right colors to support your vision of the space. Most designers suggest that earth tones and dusty greens and blues are relaxing. If your private space is a place where you want to actually accomplish things, oranges and reds are said to be energizing. I have a client with a bright pumpkin-colored office who absolutely loves her space. Working in that energetic room, she feels that she doesn't even need coffee. Pay special attention to lighting in your private spaces as well. For some, this will be an area where relaxing work such as knitting or writing or scrap booking takes place, so you will want your work area to be well lit. If this is a meditation space or just a place to "chill out," you will want to have very low lighting that can be adjusted according to your mood. Once you have chosen the color for the walls, its time to consider what to hang on them. It's nice to have coordinated frames, which give the space a more finished, peaceful look. Many people choose to hang family photos in their private spaces. This is a great idea. But exclude pictures of people who are upsetting to you. Mirrors can add a lot of ambiance to almost any space, but take note of what they reflect. If they reflect the backs of your family members busy in the next room, you might find this distracting.

Now pay attention to the storage in the space. When you walk through the room, does it seem cluttered or serene? Under-the-bed storage is tempting but can be a bad choice. Filling the space beneath where you sleep with big boxes and other items blocks the flow of *chi* and disturbs sleep. Use it for storage only as a last resort. Scan the dresser tops and other flat surfaces. They can be clutter magnets. Make sure that you have little boxes for hair bands, watches and jewelry, coins, and other items that are attracted to this spot. Chairs should not become places to pile things. Place a magazine caddy next to your reading chair; find a place to stack newspapers to recycle. When all your treasures are in place, the room still should have a sense of openness.

Consider the windows as well. For some, a great view of the yard is very soothing. On the other hand, if your view is distracting because the lawn needs mowing or the swing set is falling down, you may want window treatments to screen the view. Your private space should feel like an oasis for you. Also, don't forget texture when planning your room. A lovely soft throw on a big armchair always relaxes me. You should be able to come to this spot on even your worst day and find solace there.

How to Create Private Spaces When All Your Space Is Shared

Of course, not all of us are fortunate enough to have a whole room all to ourselves. More often bedrooms are shared, and privacy is found in areas that are not ours alone. How can you create a "room of your own" when all your space is shared with family members? Try creating zones for each member of your family. The space needs to support everyone's different energies. This is especially important in children's bedrooms. I have a boss who despises pink so passionately that he won't allow so much as a pink marker past his door jamb. Because he has a private office, this is not a problem. In a shared space, though, you'll need to make some compromises. If you have your heart set on lavender, for example, perhaps a very pale, dusty lavender with a lot of brown undertones will please both of you. There are some ultra-sophisticated lavenders that look almost like taupe and whites that carry a subtle tint of lavender. Try getting samples of a few of these to see how your roommate feels. If he or she loves green and you love lavender, paint the walls leaf green, and add some nice lavender throw pillows. Or you can paint your walls a neutral color and accent your own areas within the rooms according to your taste. White walls with chocolate-brown furniture suit most people and accommodate a variety of accent colors. Keep a small vase of lavender roses on your night stand and a lavender throw draped across your end of the bed. Our partners can choose their own accent pieces that have meaning for them as well. Ideally, your objects will blend with one another, but if not, you might consider letting your partner hang his or her prize football jersey on his or her side of the room.

An Action Plan for Bedrooms

Although bedrooms are typically the most private rooms in a house, they are very often a shared space. As I mentioned earlier, it is important to organize the bedroom in a way that makes sense for each person who lives there. If you love to read in bed but your partner hates bright lighting, put the overhead light on a dimmer, and choose a reading light (or perhaps even a book light that attaches to your book) with a focused beam that won't illuminate the entire area. Be sure to provide plenty of storage options for magazines and books if you're a reader. This can be a bookcase or simply a nice basket on the floor. Laundry can be an issue in the bedroom as well. If you are in the habit of filling your bed or your reading chair with stacks of clean laundry, you can break the cycle by making it as simple as possible to put your clothes away. Keep your drawers and closet easily accessible. If you know you won't return sweaters to a high shelf where they are stored, find another, more reachable spot for them. You also might consider purchasing an attractive large basket, one big enough to hold a load or two of folded laundry. You can tote the basket from room to room as you put items away. And if you don't get to put every item in its place immediately, you'll be looking at a pretty basket rather than an unsightly pile.

Feng Shui suggests that the "commanding position" for your bed is as far away from your bedroom door as possible, but you still should be able to see the door while lying in bed. Seeing who is coming and going is considered more relaxing. Lots of people do some of their best thinking while lounging in bed. If you like to ponder things deeply while resting in bed, you might want to consider adding some photos to your bedroom walls that will remind you of your most important goals and dreams. By keeping a tangible reminder of your most important goals in sight, you will increase your ability to visualize these positives outcomes. The more carefully you imagine them, the more quickly they will manifest for you. Your bedroom is a great place to display a picture of your mate as well because this is the space that most nurtures your relationship.

Things to toss or donate:

Torn bedding

Bedding that doesn't fit your bed

Old pillows (Pillows harbor dust mites and should be replaced every three to six months.)

Mattresses that sag or dip (Once they sag, they need to be thrown away.)

Out-of-date newspapers and magazines

Unused or underused exercise equipment

Books you don't plan to read again

Remotes or electronics that don't work

Uncomfortable chairs

Bric-a-brac (It is better to have a few meaningful objects than a dresser top loaded with stuff.)

Do you have the following?

A place for reading materials beside the bed

A hamper for dirty clothes

A place for clothes that need to be dry-cleaned

A place for clothes that need to be mended or ironed

Sufficient storage for your wardrobe

An alarm clock

A night stand, preferably equipped with a small drawer to store reading glasses, remotes, and the like

Reading lights

A small stereo or i-Pod docking station with a place to store CDs

A comfortable bed that is relatively easy to make (Do you really need so many throw pillows?)

A wastebasket

A place to sit while you put on your shoes

A full-length mirror

A phone in the bedroom (Some people feel that this is necessary for emergencies.)

A comfortable rug for bare feet at the side of the bed

A clear path to the bathroom and hall

Bedroom Problem Solvers

If you don't have room for night stands next to the bed, try a small floating shelf.

Store CDs or DVDs inside small baskets on shelves to cut down on visual clutter.

Look for multipurpose storage. Hide a TV behind the doors of an armoire, and store clothes in the drawers below. Keep a spare blanket inside an ottoman or in a blanket chest that doubles as seating at the foot of the bed.

Box spring covers that attach with Velcro can hide an ugly box spring while still allowing you to keep the space under the bed clutter free.

An Action Plan for Children's Rooms

It takes a little extra thought to make a child's bedroom or playroom function well. If your children are sharing a room, be sure to designate areas for the exclusive use of each child. At a bare minimum, each child should have his or her own bed, work area, and place to store toys and clothes. Some families designate a shelf for each child for toys that are "too special to share." Anything not on that shelf is okay for both children to use. With some adult guidance, this system can avoid a lot of squabbling. Try to arrange the space with some nooks within the room. A top bunk or a window seat tucked behind a curtain can afford your child some well-needed privacy.

If you want your children to tidy up their own rooms, it is crucial that you set up systems with them in mind. If a child can't open the drawers or reach the hanging rod in the closet, he or she can't learn to put away his or her own clothes. I would also advise against the old-fashioned "toy box" many of us were raised with. These large boxes inevitably just become an unmanageable jumble of mismatched pieces. Instead, provide smaller bins or baskets that can be organized by toy types—cars, balls, doll clothes, etc. Children can use zones too, and each activity in their room should be planned out. Look back at your vision plan for this space, and make sure that you have taken into account what you need. A small basket or box for pencils on a child's desk is helpful too. Next time you are at your child's school, take a look at the classroom. Even the youngest children's classes usually feature neatly organized shelves that are easy for a child to maintain. Everything is labeled, often with a picture as well as a word. Your child's room should be just as easy to maintain as his or her classroom.

Keep children's toys to a minimum. If you have a surplus, try storing some toys in the basement or other off-site area and then rotating them with the toys in the bedroom. When children are overwhelmed with clutter, it drains their energy just as much as it does yours. I had one friend who used to "feature" a different toy each morning on the coffee table in their great room. A toy that may have been ignored for months on the toy shelf suddenly became the belle of the ball when it was placed center stage.

Children's clothing requires a special action plan as well. Many parents find it easier for children to dress themselves if they organize their wardrobe by outfits rather than by shirts, pants, etc. You can buy one of those canvas organizers that enables you to stack an outfit for each day, or you can place outfits in clear plastic bags in your child's drawers. Each hanger can hold a complete outfit as well. It is also a good practice to remove all out-of-season clothes from your child's dresser. How many of us have been surprised by a preschooler decked out in beach garb when its twenty degrees outside?

Babies come with their own issues. When planning a nursery, it is very important to have all necessary baby supplies in easy reach. You don't want to have to leave a baby on a changing pad while you fetch the diaper cream from the other side of the room. Don't neglect lighting and noise issues as well. Some babies will sleep past sunrise only if their room is equipped with blackout shades. If your baby is a light sleeper, you might want to consider wall-to-wall carpet and hanging quilts on the walls to cut down on noise. And of course, baby-proof the space. You can never be sure when your toddler will finally find his or her way over the crib rail, so you want him or her to find a hazard-free space on the other side.

When it is time to design a child's room, try as much as possible to incorporate the child in the process. Children are better supported by a space that appeals to them visually. So even if you aren't thrilled with teal or fuchsia, it may be more important that the space be comfortable for the child than that it be designer perfect. If you aren't entirely ready to hand the kids the paint deck, you can invite them to choose the accessories. This is a great way for a child to create his or her own area within a shared space. Paint the walls a neutral color, and let each child choose pillows and bedding in a color that appeals to him or her. Wallpaper borders are an excellent solution here. They are easily removed with a damp sponge when your fairy princess morphs into a tomboy or a teenager.

There are some Feng Shui tricks you can use if you want to improve your child's sleep patterns. For children who have difficulty falling asleep, point the head of the bed North or West. For children who have difficulty waking in the morning, try facing the head of the bed East or South. This is believed to help people to rise early. If you are interested in helping your children reach their goals, you might want to consider providing them with their own private vision boards to hang in their bedrooms. They can place pictures here of all the wonderful things they want to attract into their own lives.

Things to toss, donate, or store elsewhere:

All but the most recent or most treasured school projects

Games with missing pieces

Forgotten collections

Coloring books with most pages filled

Any toy that no longer functions well enough to be played with

Anything that is dirty and can't be cleaned

Broken crayons and dried-out paints and Playdoh

Toys that the children have outgrown

Toys that are too old or complicated for the child to enjoy

Books that are no longer of interest or the right reading level

Clothing and shoes that have been outgrown

Clothing and shoes that are out of season or out of favor

Single socks and socks with holes

Stained and ripped clothing (Leave it in their room, and you know they will want to wear it!)

Toys that are too messy or noisy for the bedroom

Do you have the following?

Clothes stored in a way that allows your child to easily dress himself or herself and put the clothes away on his or her own

A hamper for dirty laundry

A lamp by the bed

A night light

A place to read comfortably with your child

Toy organizers so that like toys can be placed together

Plenty of storage space and then some

A work zone if your child does schoolwork in the room

A play zone

A resting and reading zone

A safe place to sleep

A place to display artwork, ribbons, and other treasures

Some family photos of relatives and friends who live far away (helps younger children remember them)

An Action Plan for Bathrooms

Bathroom organization is key because this area needs to function efficiently for you. Who has five extra minutes to waste in the morning looking for the right shampoo? If it's the end of the day and you have the time to soak in the tub, you want the space to be clutter-free and relaxing. Because it is important to balance all five elements in Feng Shui (earth, water, fire, air, and metal) it is a good idea to include an earth element in the bathroom, such as a live plant or a small bowl of pebbles to balance out the abundance of water in this space.

Bathrooms are often short on storage, so look for small, hidden storage opportunities. Clear plastic trays can be very useful. Is there room for a shelf or étagère behind the toilet? Can you use the windowsill to store pretty bath products? The writer Grace Paley used to tell her students that she did her best writing in the bathtub. To make your bathroom both restful and functional, organize all your supplies into zones. Keep frequently used products where they can be reached easily. You may want to consider adding a hotel-type hook on which to hang your blow-dryer or adding a small shelf above the sink for toothbrushes. If the bath is shared, then you will each want your own area in the bath. It is not fun to have to paw through five other bottles to get to your shaving cream. Within each person's space, create smaller zones organized by the item's uses. Place all your makeup together in one basket and your medications together in another. Other zones might include hair care, dental care, towels, cleaning products, and skin care. If you group like objects together within these groups, you will be in and out in no time in the morning.

Things to toss, donate, or store elsewhere:

Duplicates (Do you really need four different shampoos?)

Expired medications, both prescription and over the counter

Extra towels and bath mats

Frayed or stained towels and bath mats

Anything not regularly used in the bathroom

Old magazines, catalogues, and newspapers

Soap scraps

Out-of-date or broken appliances

Old toothbrushes

Expired or out-of-style makeup

A note on the shelf-life of cosmetics: Although cosmetic companies are not required by the U.S. Food and Drug Administration to print expiration dates on their products, cosmetics that are out of date can pose significant health risks. It is particularly dangerous to use old mascara. Some manufacturers recommend replacing mascara every three months or as soon as it becomes dry. Do not try to moisten dry mascara. You can introduce bacteria into the product. All-natural products expire more quickly than other types and need to be replaced more often. Any product that has changed in texture, separated, or has a different odor should be discarded. Liquid foundations should be replaced every three to six months. Very few cosmetics, including powders and blushes, are safe to use one year after the purchase date. Keep in mind that expiration dates are only meant to serve as guidelines; products that are exposed to excessive heat or stored improperly actually may expire well before this date.

Do you have the following?

Plenty of storage for towels (Hooks, shelves, and bars are all good—anything to prevent someone from throwing that wet towel on the bathroom floor.)

Cleaning products for each surface in the bathroom, stored in a caddy

Sufficient task lighting (Can you see well enough to apply makeup?)

A large mirror for the "big picture" and a magnifying or hand mirror for applying makeup or putting in contact lenses

A wastebasket

A place to store magazines or books if you read in your bath

A place to store shampoo and bath products in the shower or adjacent to the bath

Enough storage space for your essential daily items (You may want a separate basket or caddy just for these products that are part of your daily routine.)

An Action Plan for Closets

Our current fixation with nesting is most in evidence in our closets. New houses feature closets the size of small bedrooms. There is a reason for the walk-in closet's high appeal. A well-organized closet really does make for an easier life. There are so many options today for closet storage that there is a solution that's just right for everyone. Don't forget that clutter stashed behind closed doors still has a negative impact on your life. Clutter blocks the flow of energy within a space whether it is visible or not. Cleaning out your closet is a great way to release trapped energy in your home. Everyone's clothing storage needs are different. Someone who lives in jeans and tees is not going to need as much hanging space as someone who wears a suit to work each day. The best way to organize your closet is to do what the experts do. Take a detailed inventory of everything you currently store in your closet, and tailor your space to fit.

First, you need to pare down your wardrobe. Most of us are not blessed with abundant storage space, and at some point we all need to whittle down our possessions. A seasonal review of your wardrobe can keep your newly organized space from refilling. Storing seasonal and formal wear in another location also can free up precious space for your regular wardrobe. If you are short on hanging space, don't forget to look up. Most closets are tall enough to accommodate a double row of hanging rods. It helps to store clothes on the proper hangers so that they don't fall and to group like items together such as skirts, dresses, blouses, pants, etc. The clothes take up less space this way. Shoes need to be visible and are best stored in clear containers or on open shelves. If you can see your shoes without having to push hanging items out of the way, that's ideal. Here's a checklist to get you started.

Things to toss, donate, or store elsewhere:

Anything you haven't worn in over a year

Anything that doesn't fit—no exceptions

Anything that you can't imagine wearing

Anything that is stained, ripped, or unwearable

Clothes in a color you dislike

Gifts that are not your style

Shoes that hurt your feet or are out of style

Buying mistakes (It's better to just move on.)

Clothes that should be stored in another space—out-of-season coats, formal wear, etc.

Do you have the following?

Sufficient light inside the closet and inside your drawers (Stick-on lights run by batteries are great.)

Enough room to see each item in the closet without having to push other things aside

Shoe storage that allows you to see the shoes easily (Some models tape photos of the shoes to the outside of the box; clear plastic containers work well too.)

The right kind of hangers for each type of clothing—skirt hangers with clips, padded hangers for sweaters, etc. (Wire hangers should be avoided because they are not great for your clothes.)

Drawer inserts to keep lingerie, socks, and other items in their spots (optional)

A place to hang belts and scarves

A place to store purses and bags

Shoe-polishing supplies

An iron and ironing board either in the closet or nearby (at least on the same floor)

A valet hook (a hook to hang an outfit on before you dress or pack)

Creating a Meditation Space

We live in a very tense society. We are pulled apart . . . and we all need to learn how to pull ourselves together. . . . I think that at least part of the answer lies in solitude.

—Helen Hayes

It is only when we silence the blaring sounds of our daily existence that we can finally hear the whispers of truth that life reveals to us, as it stands knocking on the doorsteps of our hearts.

—K. T. Jong

Meditation is an ancient and sacred way to clear the clutter from your mind and allow you to focus. As I have discussed frequently throughout this book, clutter in your home environment creates a sense of clutter within yourself. To feel fully relaxed and able to set better goals for your life, it is essential to have at least one area of your home that is free from both literal and metaphorical "baggage." Once you create a space that truly supports your new goals, you will be better able to manifest positive changes. Because a meditation corner or room is a space dedicated to our spiritual well-being, it is crucial that its environment supports you completely. Be sure to consider all your senses, as well as how you like to meditate—or keep a journal, or listen to music, if these activities help you connect with your spiritual side. Some people set up their meditation corner outside in the yard. The garden can be a great place to practice "active meditation," meditation while moving or exercising. You may even want to make several little nooks to support different goals in your life, such as a special corner for abundance and another for good health. If you practice a religion, you can include a few religious objects that can serve as a focal point. Items can be placed on an altar or allowed to stand alone. However, be sure to limit yourself to just a few key pieces. This is not the place for clutter or disorder because you don't want anything to distract you while you are in your sacred space.

Candles often function as focal points in meditation rooms. If you plan to use candles in the space, be sure that the room can be darkened as completely as possible. Blue is often a popular wall color for meditation rooms because a blue background makes it easier to focus on one central object or light source. Placing a crystal or something made of crystal near a candle to refract the light is also a lovely way to create a sacred aura in a space.

If you like to have music playing while you meditate, be sure to provide a boom box, stereo, or iPod for your space. Wonderful scents can help you to concentrate as well. If you don't care for traditional incense and essential oils, you can use scented candles, flowers, or fruit. A meditation room, even if it is used for a slightly different purpose, is the most sacred space in your home, and therefore, it also should be the most personal. There are no rights and wrongs as long as the space is comfortable, organized, and visually pleasing to you. There is no need to force yourself to listen to Tibetan monks chant and light up sandalwood incense if these things take you out of your comfort zone. Feel free to make the space entirely your own because you want to spend as much time in this area as you can.

If there is light in the soul, there is beauty in the person,
If there is beauty in the person, there is harmony in the house,
If there is harmony in the house, there is order in the nation,
If there is order in the nation, there will be peace in the world.
—Chinese Proverb

Absolutely everything in the space that does not cdirectly onnect with meditating, praying, journaling, or other activities that you do to support your spiritual evolution should be tossed, donated, or stored elsewhere. It is best to avoid making your meditation space a dual-purpose area because you don't want to interrupt your concentration. If you do not have an entire room to dedicate to meditation, you can place all the objects you would like to use into a canvas bag or a backpack. You know that when you open your bag, it is time to focus. Even if you do have a dedicated meditation space at home, you still may like to have a portable meditation station that you can bring with you when you travel.

Do you have the following?

A small light source to focus on, such as a candle

Lighting that can be dimmed

Drapes to block out daylight

A crystal or a few other objects that feel spiritual to you

A comfortable place to sit (You may want a large stool with a back to support you if you plan to sit cross-legged for a long time.)

A yoga or prayer mat

An altar

A music source with appropriate CDs

A space that is spare but visually pleasing to you

A second, possibly smaller, set of meditation essentials in a bag or backpack that can travel with you

CHAPTER 7

Kitchens and Dining Rooms

Tell me what you eat, I'll tell you who you are.
—Anthelme Brillat-Savarin

Training is everything. The peach was once a bitter almond; cauliflower is nothing but cabbage with a college education.
—Mark Twain

Kitchens and dining rooms are places to nourish your family as well as your guests. For this reason, it is especially important that they be welcoming spaces. I have an open kitchen, and despite the fact that my family room and living room are lovely, the kitchen remains the heart of my home. It's where my guests congregate. A recent study estimates that the average adult spends over one thousand hours a year in the kitchen, often accompanied by the rest of the family. The kitchen also tends to be the busiest room in the house. Perhaps more than any other room, your kitchen needs to function flawlessly or it can siphon energy faster than a falling soufflé. Thus, if you have several rooms in your home that need organizing, you might want to consider tackling the kitchen first.

Since this is the room that "feeds" the family both literally and metaphorically, it is essential that it not be allowed to remain in a state of unbalance. If your kitchen and dining room are not functioning well for you, you may find that your family is not growing as well as you would like, both physically and spiritually.

A poorly arranged and messy space can cause a family to have more arguments and to feel fatigued and out of sorts. When your daughter can't find her backpack and your keys have disappeared into the junk drawer, it is unsettling to say the least. These distractions take time and energy away from the things that should be the true focus of your family—building loving relationships and evolving together to fulfill your individual callings.

Food is a source of energy; it creates the flow of energy through our bodies. When you feed your family healthy, properly prepared foods, you give them the best possible chance to manifest their most positive selves. Your cooking space should support this vital activity. As I mentioned earlier, quantum physics holds that both animate and inanimate objects are composed of little pools of dense energy waves. These waves are constantly colliding and interacting with each other. Like sound waves or water waves, when they combine, they either cancel each other out or reinforce one another. If clutter and disorganization cause you to waste a great deal of energy preparing meals, you may find yourself bereft of energy in other areas of your life. And if working in your kitchen is a frustrating experience, the food you prepare there is likely to suffer as a result.

Feng Shui recognizes the complex interplay between nourishing our bodies and nourishing other aspects of our lives. Food and its preparation are seen to have a significant impact on a family's prosperity and abundance. When you cook, various energies combine to create something new. Take a raw egg and then cook it. You will see that it is nothing like it was before. Cooking is a transformative process. Guests in your kitchen absorb the energy of everything in this space. The cook, the teapot warming on the stove, and the smell of the bread in the oven interact to create the flow and energy of the room.

Ideally, these energies will be in harmony and balance with one another. Chinese culture is more holistic than our Western culture. For centuries, the Chinese have understood that imbalance and disharmony block the flow of energy. Balance is essential to health and vitality, whether it is applied to the yin and yang of a dish or the yin and yang of a room. For the Chinese, the contrast between spicy and mild or sweet and sour foods makes for more appetizing dishes and increases health by providing diners with a balanced source of energy. The Chinese define illness as an imbalance between one of the body's systems and the body as a whole. No distinction is drawn between mental illness and physical illness either; spiritual or psychological health is irrefutably connected to physical health.

The holistic understanding of the mind–body connection also exists within the law of attraction. When you become frustrated, you project this negativity out into the room. If you are frustrated by working in a poorly organized kitchen, your family members are likely to pick up on your bad mood and internalize it to some degree. They, in turn, will reinforce the notion that the kitchen is an unhappy place and send that negativity out into the universe. And guess what? The universe responds by sending you more frustration! This is one more reason to apply a significant positive energy toward putting your kitchen and dining area in order.

Fewer Burners on the Stove Equals Fewer Dollars in the Pocket

According to Feng Shui, stovetops play a pivotal role in family health. Both the position of your stove and the numbers of burners are thought to have an impact on the material and spiritual wealth of your family. Because the stove and the burners represent wealth, Feng Shui practitioners believe it is beneficial to use your stove as frequently as possible. Extra burners promise extra wealth, so if you can afford it, go ahead and splurge on that six-burner range! If you have the standard four-burner cook top, you can increase your wealth luck by rotating burners. Using more of the burners opens more channels through which wealth can enter your home. And repair broken burners immediately because they invite economic difficulties.

In the dining room, ornate dishes and crystal glasses also carry extra wealth luck. A fun way to increase abundance for your family is to serve a lavish meal on your best china from time to time. After all, doesn't everyone feel just a little bit richer while eating an elegant dinner? The law of attraction applies here, too. If you sit down to dine in a more formal setting once in a while, you'll feel wealthier and signal the universe to provide you with more wealth. You have to feel it to receive it!

The kitchen can be the most difficult space to organize and the most likely spot to be full to the brim with stuff. Some of us have a kitchen tool for every task from whipping cream to peeling garlic. Luckily, expert kitchen designers have put a lot of thought into this already and have come up with some guidelines to help with space planning. Whether you're a five-star chef or a frozen-dinner type, below are some basic guidelines to help you conquer your kitchen and dining areas. Review these pointers in "mouse view," and then make sure to incorporate them into your vision. Next, spend as much time and energy as possible focusing on your updated vision plan for your kitchen and dining areas. Creating a space full of energy and harmony will help to generate positive change in your life as a whole.

The most remarkable thing about my mother is that for thirty years she served the family nothing but leftovers. The original meal has never been found.

—Calvin Trillin

When a Great Room's Not So Great—How to Keep Kitchen Clutter from Overwhelming Your Connected Living Space

Many people who are buying a new home today want a house featuring an open floor plan. Rooms that flow into one another work especially well for today's families, which often pursue several different activities at the same time. A parent may cook dinner while one child does homework and another works at the computer. Because leisure time is limited, we like spaces that allow us to multitask together. The great room is brilliant for this reason.

But there is a downside to this convivial setting. Each activity requires its own set of supplies. A tremendous volume of stuff is needed in this one space. A great room starts looking not so great as the clutter piles up. How easy is it for a teenager to concentrate on his science project when he is surrounded by a week's worth of mail and his sister's current scrapbook materials? Here are some simple ways to keep an open living area organized:

- Keep dirty pots and meals in progress out of view of the rest of the room by building a small six- to eighteen-inch wall down the center of the island; cooking mess stays hidden on the cooking side, but the chef can still chat freely with anyone in the room.

- Make sure that you have plenty of storage for every item that might be used in this space such as a sewing kit so that you can reattach a button while watching TV and then can store it after the job is done.

- Designate specific zones for reading, cooking, eating, TV viewing, bill paying, mud-room storage, sports equipment storage, baking, beverages, dish washing, and all the items that travel with you in and out of the house, such as keys, briefcases, and backpacks.

- Make sure that all surfaces in this heavily trafficked room, such as tile and carpet, are durable and low maintenance.

- When you create your plan of attack for this room, bear in mind the various ages and sizes of the people who are sharing the space. If you position a microwave within reach of school-age children, perhaps they can make their own breakfasts. If you or your spouse are extra tall, you may want to make countertops a few inches higher than the norm. If you have a bad back, choose a softer floor surface such as wood instead of tile. If standing is difficult for you, make sure you include a space to mix and chop while sitting down. Frequently used items should be very easy to retrieve and to store.

How to Create a Zoned Kitchen

Like the other areas of your home, kitchen and dining spaces work when zoned into different work centers. Almost every kitchen will include zones for dishwashing, food preparation, cooking, dining, and storage. Some families also may appreciate having a space dedicated to baking, coffee making, beverage storage, microwaving, bill paying, and television viewing. I have a zone just for my meal planning. Your zones will be unique to your family. To make sure that you have thought of everything, go back to your kitchen assessment and make sure that you've accounted for each activity that you do there. Concentrate on your vision for this room as well. Your ideal kitchen might include new centers that are missing from your current space. You may have to wait a while longer before you create the kitchen of your dreams, but incorporate your smaller goals (such as creating an organized space for packing school lunches or baking pies) right away. Sometimes an intent focus on your vision will uncover a simpler or more cost-effective upgrade.

How to Create a Work Triangle, Not a Bermuda Triangle, in Your Kitchen

Professional kitchen designers get paid significant fees to create kitchens that optimize traffic patterns in the work area. Some designer kitchens include every bell and whistle. However, many professionally designed spaces are quite modest in size and scope. As much as we might yearn for acres of counterspace and multiple islands, the most experienced kitchen experts will tell you that an efficient layout needn't be elaborate or massive. If you follow these guidelines by the National Kitchen and Bath Association, your kitchen will be cooking in no time.

If your kitchen is not ready for remodeling, you can still create a work triangle of your own simply by relocating some furniture and appliances. If you do replace the countertop to relocate the dishwasher, it is possible that the increased usability of the space will more than compensate for the added cost.

The *work triangle* is defined by the National Kitchen and Bath Association as an imaginary straight line drawn from the center of your sink, to the center of your cook top, to the center of your refrigerator, and finally back to the sink again. Some large kitchens may have more than one triangle. You can create additional triangles for yourself by drawing imaginary lines between any three appliances that you use in conjunction with one another such as a coffee maker, refrigerator, and sink. Here are the ideal proportions for a work triangle:

- The sum of the work triangle's three sides should not exceed twenty-six feet, and each leg should measure between four and nine feet.

- No major traffic patterns should intersect the triangle; that is, if family members have to cut through your work triangle every time they head to the back door, the efficiency of your kitchen will suffer.

- The work triangle should not cut through an island or peninsula by more than twelve inches.

- If the kitchen has only one sink, it should be located across from or in between the cooking surface, preparation area, or refrigerator.

- Entries, appliances, or cabinet doors should not interfere with each other.

- Work aisles should be at least forty-two inches wide for one cook or forty-eight inches wide for two cooks.

Don't despair if you can't create an ideal work triangle in your own space right now. These are useful guidelines, but even the professionals break the rules on occasion. Feel free to make your own choices. In particular, it can be difficult to adhere to a triangular plan if you have a very large kitchen or a kitchen that is being used simultaneously by two or more cooks. In instances where it isn't possible to construct the perfect triangle, you can make the most of your space by creating a zoned kitchen with activities such as dish washing, food preparation, and cooking concentrated in specific areas. Make sure that all related supplies are within easy reach inside these zones.

> *All sorrows are less with bread.*
> —*Miguel de Cervantes*, Don Quixote

Keeping Conversation Flowing—How to Organize a Dining Room for Entertaining

No family wants to be sidetracked by clutter and disorder when sitting down to dine, whether the "dining room" is in a corner of a room or an elegant space all its own. Here are some guidelines to keep in mind if you want your dining room to be as comforting as the food you serve there:

- Good news for collectors: The dining room is often a great space to display all those vintage teapots or signed baseballs. The key is to make the displays interesting but not distracting or overwhelming to the space. Try stashing everything in a curio cabinet or displaying collectibles on matching floating shelves along one wall of the room.

- Windows should allow in lots of natural light but also have some drapes or blinds for controlling glare if this is an issue.

- Your table and chairs should be comfortable. You want your guests to linger. There should be room at the table for each place setting to have twenty-four inches of tabletop, and there should be eighteen inches from the last setting to the end of the table.

- Plan to allow at least three feet from the back of a chair to the wall to allow diners to pull their chairs in and out comfortably.

- Have lighting that can be altered to suit the mood of the moment.

- A beautiful or interesting centerpiece is necessary, but feel free to be creative. When featured at the center of a dining table, lots of everyday objects can look impressive. A glass bowl filled with apples can be every bit as enticing as a silver vase full of expensive flowers. Avoid centerpieces that block diners' views of each other. Everyone at the table should be able to look at one another without obstruction.

- Mirrors and candles are lovely in the dining room and are believed to stimulate conversation.

- When you eliminate distractions in the dining room, you strengthen the ties between the people at the table.

CHAPTER 8

Home Offices

Home ought to be our clearinghouse, the place from which we go forth lessoned and disciplined, and ready for life.
—Kathleen Norris

Any intelligent fool can make things bigger, more complex, and more violent. It takes a touch of genius—and a lot of courage—to move in the opposite direction.
—E. F. Schumacker

Be content with what you have, rejoice in the way things are. When you realize there is nothing lacking, the whole world belongs to you.
—Lao Tzu

The home office has become command central for many families these days. With everyone rushing off in many different directions, keeping track of each person's schedule can require an advanced degree in time management. It was not so very long ago that families woke with the sun, worked until the sun set, cooked dinner, cleaned up, and went to bed. A whole day could pass in this manner without encountering any paperwork whatsoever! How times have changed. We now dash from work to the gym, from school to soccer, from housework to volunteering, and each one of these activities comes with a pile of paperwork attached. In addition, there is all the virtual paper to consider. If you are to have any hope of keeping up with it all, you will need a system for organizing your virtual office as well as your physical office. This chapter will cover all of this in detail.

An office extends beyond the physical space it occupies. Whether you work in an armchair with a laptop perched over your knees or in a large office of your own, the ease with which you accomplish things has a profound impact on the rest of your life. When you struggle to complete everyday tasks, it very difficult to stay positive about the big picture. How can you focus on improving your career or your relationships when you have to expend undue energy finding the scissors and locating that memo you meant to read? It's nearly impossible. Not only will tasks take longer to complete, but your focus on the disorder of your space will draw more mess and clutter into your life. It is very important to break bad habits as soon as possible so that you can free yourself from this chaotic cycle. After all, like attracts like. What you focus on expands to fill the space in your head—and the space in your house as well.

If you find yourself continually frustrated by the circumstances surrounding your office, ask yourself what you can change to improve the situation. One way to change your focus so that you are working toward a positive goal is to place an object related to your goals in your workspace. Position it so that you will see it on a daily basis. Each time you see a picture of what you want to draw to you, you reinforce your commitment to that goal. Encourage family members to try the same thing. You can create a bulletin board that features family goals, or each member can have his or her own visual cue. If a task at hand seems impossible, instead of telling yourself that it can't be done, ask what you can do differently so that it *can* be accomplished. Quantum organizing is based on the principle that the environment you create in your head is what you create in your life. If you allow yourself to be overwhelmed by unpaid bills and unanswered e-mails, you are telling the universe that you can't stop thinking about those unpaid bills. The universe hears you and sends more bills to pay! If you can change the tape that's playing in your head, you can change your life. This is an absolute fact.

And so it is especially important that you create an office that is comfortable for you. Your office should be welcoming and comfortable because you want to enjoy spending time in there. If the environment is supportive, the quality of your work will improve. Make sure that you have a comfortable desk chair. Resist the temptation to place your office in that dreary basement corner because you can't think of anything else to do with the space. You have important work to do. Why stick yourself in an uninspiring place? The results are quite predictable. You'll spend less time working and therefore accomplish less. If you can, set up your office in the front of the house close to where the energy enters the home. It is difficult for *chi* to flow downward, another reason a basement office is not ideal. If the basement still remains your best option, be sure to make the space as cozy as you can by providing adequate lighting and some warm touches such as live plants and evocative art. Try to find room for a comfortable reading chair in addition to your desk chair. It's great to have a more contemplative spot to go to when you need to recharge at work. Other people may prefer to recharge their batteries on a treadmill or by donning headphones. I've read about one productive billionaire who does most of his work while riding a stationary bike! The important thing is to organize your space so that it works for your own unique work style. It doesn't need to be conventional— it just needs to work for you.

A home office is high on many people's wish list, even those who already have an office away from home. If your floor plan won't accommodate a separate room for your home office, a small nook in another room can function perfectly well. When you are deciding where to locate your office, consider the traffic patterns in the rest of the house. Do you need to be in the hub of your home so that you can monitor young children while you work, or will you be happier positioning yourself far from hub? If the office is to be a shared space, is it easily accessible to everyone who uses it? If you will be paying your bills in the office, is it close to the spot where the mail is delivered? If not, you will want to make sure that you have a system in place for transferring the mail from the front door to your in-box.

Once you have decided on the ideal location for your office, go back to your vision plan and review your assessment for this space. Put yourself back in "mouse view" for a few minutes, and determine what you need to do to make that vision a reality. Do you have all the pieces of furniture you need? Do you have a furniture plan in mind that will work? More than in any other room in the house, be very specific about what you need when it comes to storage. Even if you aren't a list maker, you may want to make a list of the different types of paperwork you do and then make sure that you have enough file space or shelf space to accommodate it.

If you're not a fan of file cabinets, there are lots of other clever ways to organize paperwork. One of my clients swears by file boxes she stores on shelves. This suits her own work habits beautifully because when she is working on a particular task such as compiling her taxes or filling out the kid's lunch menus, she can remove the box that holds the relevant information and take it with her to the kitchen or family room. With a system this portable, her office travels with her. I know other people who absolutely swear by the piles system of paper management. This may not be the most aesthetically pleasing path to take, but if you know what is in each pile and can find your papers without wasting time, there is nothing wrong with piles. If you are a big piler, remember to incorporate lots of shelves into your plan. When you can't back up your desk chair without toppling your health records, you have a problem. There is no right or wrong way to organize an office as long as you can function efficiently in the space.

The adage "time is money" is true for many of us. We constantly try to squeeze extra work into our already hectic lives. If you find you waste a great deal of time hunting for relevant documents, you are squandering your most valuable asset—spare time.

Setting Up Systems and Handling Paperwork

It is a challenge to keep work organized at home. My biggest problem at the moment is my kitten, who loves to pounce on my papers and strew them all over the floor. I've had to adjust my systems to accommodate her. You will find that as your life evolves, you will need to update your systems from time to time. So it is best not to be overly rigid when you are setting things up in the first place. Flexible systems and simplicity will serve you well. Overly elaborate filing systems are usually quickly abandoned. If your "to file" pile keeps growing because it takes a great deal of effort to put things away, it's probably time to tweak your setup. Try to have a spot in easy reach of your desk chair for each item that you regularly encounter while at work, such as bills, forms, tax documents, catalogues, invoices, assignment letters, and so on. Desk papers are like snowflakes—no two piles are identical. There are a few organizing tools that almost everyone needs. I recommend an in-box or basket for "action items" that need to be addressed and turned around quickly. I also have a "do not lose this" basket in my office where I keep my pending paperwork. When I was researching garage door openers, I kept all the manufacturers' brochures and price lists in this basket. Once I decided on the opener I wanted, I pitched all of it.

For some people, three folders—in, out, and pending—can handle the bulk of their work. Others will require a more elaborate arrangement. The trick is to find what works for you and then maintain it.

I can't stress enough how important it is to prune your in-box, to-do lists, and your files on a regular basis. Experts estimate that 80 percent of the paperwork we carefully file away is never looked at again. If I had made a permanent file for all that garage door opener research, who knows how many years it would have sat in the drawer taking up valuable filing space. In fact, I recently found an entire file full of knitting patterns for baby clothes. My daughter is now in college. It felt great to pitch that file! If things have gotten a little out of control at your house as well, there is no need to chastise yourself too harshly. Instead, just take a deep breath and remember the ultimate goal you have for yourself. Imagine your desk completely clear of clutter. Then set aside a big chunk of time or a little time every day, and whittle away at the mess until you finally get there. Next, decide when you will go through and weed things out again. Make a plan, and whether it is daily, weekly, or monthly, and stick with it.

Even for those of us who love e-mail and BlackBerries and virtual filing, there is still a shockingly large volume of old-fashioned paper moving through the average home. Addressing this mountain of unruly pulp will separate the mice from the men. Again, efficient systems are essential. At the very least, everyone should have one safe place to keep vital documents such as wills, deeds, birth certificates, legal documents, and insurance policies. Many people will choose to keep these documents in a fireproof box or a safe deposit box at the bank. This is good foresight. In an emergency, you will want to be able to locate these documents quickly and safely. If you have to flee your home because of a natural disaster, having access to your insurance policies, Social Security cards, and bank accounts can make all the difference. Don't forget to include copies of your most current prescriptions as well if you are on medication that must be taken regularly. The people who have bothered to gather these things ahead of time will be the first ones to receive those insurance claim checks. Another good idea is to file like papers with like papers. I keep all my utilities information in one folder. All my daughter's school-related papers go into another file. Broad categories tend to work best. If you have more than a dozen or so files for your personal papers, you probably need to consolidate. But always feel free to create systems that work for you, even if they might seem a bit quirky to someone else.

My job requires extensive travel. I do not want to lose my hotel confirmation numbers or my flight information, so I have created my own system for keeping this information in one spot. For each trip, I put all my travel documents into a clear plastic sleeve that I can then slip into the folder I have created for the job site I am going to visit. This way everything is in one place, and it's very easy to walk out the door in the morning. If I have two trips close together, then I will fill a plastic sleeve for each one and place them in their separate job-site folders. I pop them into my computer bag on Sunday night before I leave. And if I have a problem with a hotel reservation, I can locate the confirmation number in just a few seconds. Simple systems like these can go far toward keeping you organized, and you won't waste psychic energy worrying about lost papers. It all comes back to making your life function optimally so that you can reserve your energy for more exciting things than keeping track of paperwork.

The Paperless Office

With all the talk of global warming and wasted resources, many concerned homeowners are trying to conserve paper and ink at home. We now think twice before printing out that ten-page e-mail. This is good for the *chi* in our homes as well. Fewer piles of paper means less clutter and fewer places in the office for valuable energy to stagnate. However, just because a report is on your laptop instead of next to it doesn't mean that there is no organizing to be done. A messy desktop on your computer can be every bit as annoying and potentially disruptive as the mess on your desk. Discard your junk e-mails as quickly as you throw away the paper junk mail that arrives in your mailbox.

It can be useful to streamline paperwork by completing tasks on-line. Shared on-line calendars that let everyone view and update them are a great help to families that need to coordinate multiple appointments. Some families get creative by making one master birthday calendar for their extended family. Paying my bills on-line has proved a wonderful time saver, and for those of us who are a little forgetful, we can receive e-mail reminders so that we don't miss an important event or a mortgage payment. Bookkeeping is far simpler with a basic on-line bookkeeping program, and you don't need an accounting course to learn to keep a ledger on your desktop. The programs offer prompts that vastly simplify the process. But you do need some discipline to maintain these systems.

However, keeping vital documents such as medical records and financial papers on your hard drive can be dangerous. As you know, computers can do something that desk's rarely do—crash! Many people have suffered a catastrophic loss of vital work because of a mysterious computer meltdown. If you decide to store important papers on your computer, it is critical that you regularly back up your work. There are several simple methods to do this. For a small monthly fee, you can gain access to a server such as imac.com that automatically backs up your work for you. You can also buy a small portable hard drive that plugs into the USB port on your computer. These removable drives are no bigger than a Post-It note pad but can store tremendous amounts of material. You can also e-mail yourself important documents or burn them onto a DVD. Whatever method you choose, you will still need to do frequent purges and occasionally delete material that you have backed up.

Shared Office Space

When an office is being shared by two or more people, special care needs to be taken so that the space will work equally well for all who use it. One of my first suggestions is to purchase a set of basic supplies for each person. Nothing is more aggravating than reaching for the scissors or tape and coming up empty handed. Having separate supplies for each person can go a long way toward maintaining family harmony. Each individual will need a storage area of his or her own as well, whether it is a cubby or an entire desk.

Sometimes a shared office isn't located inside an office at all. If your work space is the kitchen counter or the dining room table, you will want to provide a storage container for each person who works there. Make an iron-clad rule that everything goes back in the basket when a work session is finished. You should never have to push your files aside to make way for your dinner plate!

Today, when families are often challenged to find time to spend together, sitting down to do paperwork actually can be a fun bonding time. Architects and interior designers are increasingly asked to design "homework studios" or family offices for just this purpose. As long as you need to be monitoring homework, why not pay the bills at the same time? These rooms can be complete with custom built-ins and hi-tech wiring, but you can create an equally functional room for your family with just a simple desk from Ikea and some baskets for storage. It can be fun to work together. It fosters a feeling of togetherness when children see that Mom and Dad have homework too. There is no need to send the children to their rooms. In fact, bedrooms are actually one of the worst locales for a work space because bedrooms should be dedicated solely to relaxation.

If your office does double duty as a dining room or a guest room, do your assessment with that in mind. Can the messy paperwork be hidden away quickly when a friend drops by unexpectedly? Office armoires are ideally suited for this purpose, and their drawers can be used for either office supplies or linens and clothes. As I have mentioned several times before, clutter traps energy. Dining together with friends is such a wonderful way to recharge. You don't want your open box of tax files to become the black hole at the dinner party.

Everything in Its Place: What to Keep Where

There are some items almost every office contains, such as scissors, tape, an appointment book, and to-do lists. Here are some logical places to store the items that you need most frequently:

Bills to be paid—in a file folder or basket or on bulletin board if you pay frequently

Pens, pencils, scissors, stapler—in a decorative container, drawer, or pencil cup

Extra paper and ink for computer—in a box or drawer, on a shelf, or in a closet near the printer

Phone numbers and addresses—inside your computer, on a personal digital assistant (PDA), or on a bulletin board

Calendar or appointment book—if it is for multiple people, one central board with Post-Its works; for individuals, on a dry erase board or in an appointment book or on a PDA, or computer

To-do lists—one master list on your desktop or on a bulletin board or multiple lists—home, school, work—in a small binder or notebook

Some Good Floor Plans for Offices

Just as with kitchens, there are a few typical floor plans that tend to work well for office layouts. The three most popular plans are as follows:

1. Positioning a credenza behind and parallel to the desk; a second credenza can be placed in front of the desk for even more storage

2. An L-shaped desk or work space

3. A U-shaped desk or work space

When choosing a floor plan, here are a few other tips you may want to keep in mind. It is considered bad Feng Shui to have your back to the entrance to the office. This makes good practical sense as well. It is unsettling to have people enter unseen. You also may want the added security of having a solid wall behind your chair.

Consider the lighting. Natural light is always a plus, but position your computer so that glare will not be an issue. Finally, you want to be able to reach all your most important tools while seated in your desk chair. Your files, phone, computer, printer, fax machine, and whatever else you use regularly should be within arm's reach.

Thinking Outside the Box: Unconventional Storage Ideas

It isn't necessary to spend a fortune to create a well-functioning office. You can usually fulfill your office wish list with items you already have around the house. Need extra work space? A folding card table or a TV tray can fill the bill, at least temporarily. I have two old-fashioned oak ice boxes that I use for storage. I keep them stacked one on top of the other, but if I were to place them side by side they would make a great credenza. Floating shelves can work wonders when floor space needs to be kept clear. Don't forget to use all the vertical space in a room too. If you are lucky enough to have high ceilings, there is no reason not to use the extra wall space. A rolling library ladder is a handsome way to access tall shelves, but a lightweight folding ladder that can slip into a closet works equally well.

Custom built-ins are the ultimate office luxury, but I have seen people replicate this high-end look quite successfully with stock kitchen cabinets from Ikea, Home Depot, or Lowes. Not only will you find reasonable pricing, but a staff designer can do a sample layout of your space for a nominal fee or sometimes for free.

Do you have the following?

A place to store paper supplies near the printer and desk

A place to store ink for the printer and plenty of extra cartridges

A comfortable desk (If you are unusually short or tall, consider a desk that is height adjustable.)

A comfortable, ergonomic desk chair

A desk lamp

Plenty of space to store your paperwork and a system for storing it

A clock

A stereo system if you like music while you work

Lots of work space for spreading out big projects

Plenty of desk supplies—pens, paper, pencils, Post-It notes, stapler, scissors, file folders

A place to hold meetings if this is something you do or at least a guest chair

A rug to absorb sound within the space

Natural lighting or at least several sources of artificial light

A computer or legal pads—whatever you use to generate work

Scratch paper and paper on which to write to-do lists, track phone calls, etc.

Things to toss, donate, or store elsewhere:

Bills that are more than one year old and don't relate to taxes

Canceled checks that have no tax implications

Canceled checks and receipts that are more than seven years old

Tax returns and records of IRA contributions (keep permanently)

Retirement/401(k) statements (Keep until you receive the annual statement, check the transactions, and if everything is accounted for, you can shred the monthly plans and save just the annual reporting; keep these until you close the account.)

Brokerage account statements (Keep until you sell the securities; you need the purchase and sales information to prove whether you have capital gains or losses.)

Bills (These can be thrown away in most cases once the canceled check that relates to the bill has been returned; however, bills for large or expensive purchases should be kept so that the items' value can be proven if a question of insurance comes up.)

Credit card receipts (Keep until you can compare them to your statement; after that, you only need to save the receipts that have tax implications.)

Receipts for any big home improvements (Keep until you sell the house; you need a record of how much you have spent repairing and maintaining your home for tax purposes when you sell.)

CHAPTER 9

Garages, Basements, and Attics

My second favorite household chore is ironing. My first being hitting my head on the top bunk bed until I faint.
—Erma Bombeck

I think it's in my basement. . . . Let me go upstairs and check.
—M. C. Escher

There is a very good reason that closets are often referred to as a treasure trove of our deepest darkest secrets. You can "keep things in the closet," "come out of the closet," or live a "closeted life." Closets are where we hide all the stuff, both material and metaphorical, that we are not quite ready to address. Sadly, for many of us, our attics, basements, garages, and other storage areas are generally the biggest closets in our homes. Often these areas become enormous repositories for all our cast-off stuff. On a conscious level, we recognize that clutter is impeding our progress, so we dutifully remove it. Instead of eliminating it, though, we shuttle it off to the garage or the basement. Off site, out of mind! But if you have made it this far in this book, then you can guess what I am going to say next. Merely moving your junk out of sight is not a solution. If you are truly committed to securing quantum change in you life, you will need to finally clear the cobwebs and the broken appliances, rusty tools, outgrown toys, etc. from these rooms. I have one friend who recently had a Feng Shui expert analyze her home. This expert quickly realized that my friend's messy, unheated pantry, stuffed to the brim with out-of-season shoes, empty boxes, and cast-off appliances, sits squarely in the "money sector" of her home. This may be your situation as well. There is no telling what kind of positive energy—and therefore positive change—is now trapped behind the clutter in the back of your attic.

Clearing these spaces also will allow you to finally clear your conscience. Many of you started this journey toward quantum order riddled with guilt. You were ashamed of your homes and embarrassed by how difficult it was to accomplish simple tasks in these spaces. Now things have changed! If you have cleared the clutter from the bulk of your home, congratulations! However, now is not the time to rest on your laurels. Until you complete this process of reorganizing, you will not be able to truly reap the rewards for what you have carefully sown. There will always be a little whisper of dissatisfaction that remains. I want to stress that this little bit of unease really does matter. As long as you continue to worry, even just a little, about the piles in the basement, you will continue to attract more little piles. The universe does not recognize the difference between worries and wishes; if you dwell on the unhappy situation in your garage, you will attract more disorder into your life. What a shame after all your hard work! Don't jeopardize your progress in this way. Many disorganized people have difficulty finishing things. They will be doing dishes and get down to the very last pot and then leave it in the sink. Clearing your storage areas is incredibly liberating. I promise that you will be rewarded beyond measure if you just stick with this program and clear the clutter from these last few areas.

Some of you even may choose to tackle these problem areas first, and this can be an excellent choice. By clearing out your basement and your attic before you clear the rest of the house, you will be able to establish early on exactly how much storage space you have in your house. When it is time to move all the misplaced items in your main living areas, you will know exactly how many of these items are likely to fit. If you know from the beginning that there are only two empty shelves in the basement to store your extra knickknacks, you may be a bit more ruthless in your clutter clearing from the outset.

Feng Shui practitioners will tell you that there are several very sound reasons to address the clutter in your attic, basement, and garage. When clutter fills your attic, you will feel the pressure of all that stuff quite literally "hanging over your head." Some of these items may be family treasures; the attic is traditionally considered the area of your home where ancestors' issues reside. If you have had a rocky relationship with a relative and you are now storing some of his or her cast-offs in your attic, the negative energy associated with this relationship may flow to you and block more positive gains in your life. The basement, on the other hand, is thought of as the place where all our subconscious issues settle. This is definitely not the place to store all your unfinished projects! If you have lots of half-completed projects and unorganized paperwork stored there, these items are going to continue to weigh on you even if you are unaware of their presence in your thoughts.

The garage and, more specifically, the car represents freedom of movement. If your garage is dirty and poorly organized, you may find yourself feeling stagnant or stuck in place. By clearing the mess out of this area, you are freeing up the positive energy you need to make lasting changes.

In addition to the emotional importance of these areas, there are also practical reasons why these areas are so problematic for many of us. Because these areas are clutter magnets, they are often areas of our homes that we try to avoid. We prefer to zip in, grab the item we need, and go. When we can do this, fine. This is exactly how these areas should function. These are not spots for lingering. However, often we are zipping out of our basements because we don't want that pile of sports equipment to topple onto our heads! If this is the situation you are facing, here are some suggestions to help you get started.

The first priority is to purge these areas because they tend to be dumping grounds. Place like items, such as lawn tools, yard toys, seasonal decorations, etc., together so that you can create eventual zones for yourself. Ideally, you will be able to take everything out of the immediate area you are organizing and create piles for your categories nearby. This will give you the space you need to work. Then assess whether or not the area requires additional storage containers such as shelves and the like. You might want to consider purchasing additional tall garbage cans to store sports equipment and yard equipment. If you are storing anything toxic such as paints and solvents, you will want to include a lockable storage unit in your plan. Additional shelves can help you use all your available vertical space. If you are storing furniture, don't forget to use the space that is inside dresser drawers and trunks. These are the perfect places to stash paintbrushes and the like. Empty suitcases can store off-season clothes. But avoid the temptation to keep stuff just because you have a little extra storage room. When every storage area is full, there is no room to bring anything new into your life. Many of us remember the good feeling we had when we moved to a larger space and did not have every closet packed to the brim. There was a wonderful sense of expansiveness and possibility. My hope is that by making a quantum change, you will be able to recapture this feeling again in your current space.

Safety and convenience also will be paramount in your organizational schemes for these areas. Don't pile boxes so high that the items inside are inaccessible to you without a ladder, unless these are things you need only very rarely. Most important, don't forget to label things. Labels should be easily legible from wherever you will be standing to read them. For safety reasons, you will not want to store items around water heaters, dryers, and furnaces. Keep boxes and furniture a good distance away from these heat sources. Finally, when you are deciding where items should be placed, don't forget to store the most used items in front and the least used items higher up or in back. If you have to routinely rearrange your space to remove something, this is a sure sign that you still have too much stuff! Go back and reassess what is expendable. Once you have finished all this hard work, don't forget to take note of these positive changes because positive energy feeds on itself. Go ahead and drive your car in and out of the garage a few times if it pleases you. Now that the car can move freely, you are free to move on as well into a more positive place in your evolving life.

Things to toss, donate, or store elsewhere:

Broken toys

Broken sports equipment or equipment that is the wrong size

Rusted tools

Old newspapers

Broken planters and hoses

Dried-out paint

Dried-out cleaning products

Stiff paintbrushes

Weather-damaged items

Hardened putty

Diseased holiday wreaths and damaged decorations

Keys that are no longer used

Extra parts or spare parts that are no longer needed

Do you have the following?

A clear path to all your zones

Good task lighting and good general lighting

Plenty of shelves, bins, trash cans, and containers for storage

Like items stored with like items

Items stored closest to where they are used

Labels that are easy to spot and easy to read, even from a distance

A simple way to access everything that is stored in this space and a simple way to return items to this spot

Waterproof storage containers for damp areas

Acid-free tissue paper and containers for special prints and expensive clothes

A dehumidifier and a fan for damp areas

A system for removing standing water in case of floods

Lockable cabinets for power tools, flammable liquids, and other dangerous items

Plenty of open floor space to accommodate the activities that take place in this room

A chair to sit in while rummaging through boxes in search of items

A system in place for filing and preserving valuable documents and photos

A system in place for rotating clothes in and out of storage on a seasonal basis

A plan to eliminate drastic temperature changes as much as possible where valuables are stored

Divide and Conquer: How to Solicit Help from Your Team

Just the idea of organizing a garage or a basement can cause most of us to shudder. These areas tend to be large projects, and therefore, they are ideally suited to a team approach. Here are a few thoughts to keep in mind when you want to enlist some help from your family and friends:

- Prepare in advance of the big day. Make sure that you have all the organizers you need on hand and, if possible, installed before your crew arrives.

- If you anticipate throwing away or donating a large number of items, make sure that you have plenty of boxes and garbage bags to accommodate them. You also may want to call ahead and arrange for your items to be picked up the next day. This is a good way to ensure that none of these items will slowly creep back into the house!

- Make sure that you pick a date that works not only for you but for all your helpers and that they understand the scope of this project. Be clear about how many hours you hope they will be available and what time they are expected to arrive.

- Make sure that the rest of your friends and family know that you will be busy. Turn off your phone if you have to. You are the crew leader, and if you leave for even a short time, you endanger the whole project.

- Make sure that tasks are age-appropriate. Children under the age of seven or eight will not have the stamina to tackle huge piles or sort for more than an hour or so at a time. The very youngest can be given simple tasks so that they feel included, but you also may want to have someone on hand to baby-sit so that you are not constantly sidetracked by a toddler.

- Make sure that you reward your hardworking crew! Organizing needn't be drudgery. In fact, if you have children, it is highly important that you make this as positive an experience as you can and allow them to have a sense of accomplishment when its done. Your positive attitude will really pay off the next time you want them to clean their room! It can be fun to have music playing, and you also should provide drinks and snacks as well as frequent breaks for everyone involved.

- When the job is finished, show your appreciation. Treat everyone to dinner, or let everyone keep a special item. Sending flowers or a thank-you card is an unexpected courtesy that will surely be appreciated.

Note that for basements, attics, and garages, cardboard storage boxes should not be used. These areas are often damp and prone to visits by pests and insects. Mice love cardboard; it is a very cozy nesting material for them. Many insects can live off of ingested cardboard. Water can soak through it and create mold problems. Watertight containers are always the way to go for these locations. If rodents are a problem, pack your items in mouseproof containers. If you live in a warm or hot climate, Rubbermaid bins are more suitable. Also use containers made of a clear material that allows you to quickly see what is stored inside.

An Action Plan for Attics

The main hazard in attics is the tendency to overstuff the space. If you can see an item when it is stored, you can find it when it is needed. If something is hidden behind other boxes, there is a much smaller likelihood that it will be pulled out and put into service when the time comes. I have often heard people complain that they have lost entire collections of photographs or holiday ornaments only to have them turn up when they clear the attic.

When an attic is properly organized, it can become a useful multipurpose area. If you can discipline yourself to make do with less, you can easily create a cozy reading nook in your attic (especially good if you are also storing a collection of books in the space). This is also a popular space to add an extra bathroom or carve out a small guest bedroom. If this is your dream, you will want to plan for these multiple functions from the outset. Review the assessment chapter if you feel that you need some guidance in creating work zones. Here you will most likely have storage zones combined with some other sort of living space.

Sloping walls and ceilings are part of the charm and the challenge of creating useful space in an attic. Storage cubes work well here because the height of the shelving can be varied to fit these unusual wall configurations. If you are storing keepsakes to give your children at a later time, be sure to label every box so that it can be identified easily. It is best if you can leave some empty space in these containers initially because you will be adding to these collections.

Attics in some parts of the country can be either very hot or very cold. For this reason, care should be taken not to store certain items in this space. It is a good idea to avoid storing photos, slides, film footage, digital or music tapes, and the like in the attic. If your attic is not climate-controlled, these items may not survive the temperature changes. Make sure that the attic is well lit so that you can find items easily. Battery-powered lights that attach to the wall work well here or even a flashlight resting at the entrance. Adding insulation to the ceiling can help you both to save money on your heating and air-conditioning bills and to preserve the stored items. Attics also need to be ventilated. Ventilation and insulation work together to mitigate temperature swings.

An Action Plan for Garages

In the garage, you will want to maximize your vertical storage options so that the garage can still accommodate the car. Keep the floor space clear to prevent the car from damaging the stored items. Garage organizing expert Bill West notes, "If its on the floor, its time to store." In many older neighborhoods, small, detached garages are common. These little outbuildings are even more likely to become a storage unit rather than a home for the car.

Hanging cabinets can be a great option in the garage, and tall yard tools and sports equipment can be stored underneath. Many people choose to line garage walls with pegboard. The advantage of this system over installing hooks and shelves directly into your walls is its flexibility. If you acquire a new tool, you simply need to move a hook or two, and you have a spot for it. Pegboard is very inexpensive, too. Julia Childs was so enamored with pegboard that she lined her kitchen walls with it. She could certainly afford something more high end, but she could never quite convince herself to give up this system for storing kitchen utensils. Newer systems are available that come in large panels with horizontal grooves. Hooks of differing lengths fit into the grooves.

As in every other room in the house, you will want to organize your garage into work zones. All your lawn and gardening equipment should go in one area, sports equipment and car care supplies in another. Hazardous and flammable materials such as fertilizers and gasoline should be stored in a locked cabinet. Antifreeze is toxic to pets, and some pets find the stuff irresistible, so keep it locked away. If your garage is detached, this is the best place to store hazardous materials because you lessen the risk of creating a fire inside your home. Power tools are also dangerous in the wrong hands and should be locked up. Store items as close as possible to where they will be used—garden tools near the door, for example, and car repair tools alongside the car. Items should be accessible to the people who use them, too. There is no point in storing the bats and balls in a place that is out of reach of the children. Bikes should be placed close to the garage doors. There are lots of bike racks that have been developed for just this purpose. I would recommend not locating bikes behind your car to prevent damage to the car. It is too easy to accidentally scrape the car's paint when removing the bikes. Sports equipment should be secured so that it does not accidentally fall under the car.

Professional mechanics keep their tools in wheeled carts. Castors can be a great solution in a residential garage. When you need more room to paint shutters or work on the car, you can simply roll your storage unit out of your way. A garden trolley can be wheeled directly into the garden. Smaller sets of supplies, such as a pruner, trowel, and gloves or paint brushes and rags, can be stored in totes and hung on wall hooks. Now when you need to weed or touch up your trim, you can just grab the canvas bag and go straight to work.

If you plan on storing grass seed or bird feed in your garage, use tightly sealed containers to keep rodents away. As with the basement, the garage is not the place for cardboard boxes because rodents can chew their way inside or a heavy rain can turn the boxes into a pulpy mess.

There are some clever tips you can use to maximize the usefulness of your garage space. One area often neglected is the space right in front of the car. Most garages are long enough to accommodate a car and still have several feet to spare. This is a great spot for a workbench. Pull the car out into the driveway and you have plenty of room to work, and your tools are right where you need them. Equip your space with a power strip for recharging tools and a magnetic strip for holding tools at the ready, and you have everything you need to tackle a repair project. The area behind the car also can be a great place to store seasonal decorations or patio furniture. Some people may want to use this area for the recyclables as well, but if possible, these items are best stored on the sides of the garage where they can be pulled directly out to the curb without your also having to move the car.

I say "pulled" because you definitely want to consider a wheeled container for any trash that needs to move to the driveway or the curb for pickup. A shelf placed above your cans can hold important supplies such as trash bags.

Several companies sell systems that maximize the storage potential of your garage's eaves as well. Many items can be stored in the rafters or in containers that raise and lower. This is the ideal area to place seldom-used items.

If you have more to store than your garage will accommodate, you can purchase a closet for your garage! Simple outbuildings or tool sheds are available in many styles and at a range of prices. If you have the yard space, this can be a great way to increase your storage options. For short-term extra storage, several companies deliver and pick up large containers, most of which are the size of a U-Haul van and big enough to walk inside. You can pack these storage units with objects you can store off-site. Once the container has been filled, the company stores it for you in a locked storage center. This is a great time saver for those of us who feel overwhelmed by the process of uncluttering.

An Action Plan for Basements

Basements are often multipurpose areas, so you need to make sure that items don't stray from their proper zones, making the space unworkable. The treadmill or exercise bike buried under boxes has become such a familiar image that it is now a cliché. There is no point in carefully labeling and storing belongings if they are then allowed to spread like weeds into the rest of the house. If you have a play area, a TV area, or a home gym in your basement, you will want to put as much care in to maintaining these "rooms" as you do upstairs. Be sure to map out clear zones for each activity that takes place here. You will need to create storage zones as well. Like items should be stored together. There is nothing more annoying than starting to decorate the Christmas tree, only to discover that the tree topper is in a different box that can no longer be located. When you are choosing what goes where, it is a good idea to put more frequently used items in the most accessible spots.

In many parts of the country, moisture is also a problem in basements. Choose your storage containers carefully to ensure that the stored items remain dry. Dampness is the enemy. Damp items can become moldy and compromise the air quality of your entire home. Basements generally are not the best place to store out-of-season clothing and extra linens. These items will fare better in the attic, which is likely to be drier. However, if the basement is your only option for fabrics, you can protect them by storing them in airtight containers with cedar blocks or moth balls. Only use moth balls if there are no children or pets in your home. Moth balls look an awful lot like big gumballs or jaw-breakers to some young children, but they are highly poisonous. Photographs and other precious paper-based objects are equally ill suited to basement storage. These fragile materials mold and mildew very easily in a damp basement.

If you are considering setting up a home office in the basement, you may want to reconsider. Typically, energy enters your house through the front door and flows upward. The basement is the least likely room in your house to have a good productive energy flow. If the basement is the only space available to you, however, you can make the best of it by painting the walls white, making sure that you have very good lighting, and using a fan to move air and energy through your space.

Metal or plastic shelving is the best bet for basement storage because wood shelving can hold moisture and then create mold. If you use a wooden shelving unit, you may want to purchase little plastic covers for the feet, which will give you a few inches of water protection in the case of a flood. If your basement has a tendency to produce puddles, you will want to store only waterproof items on the bottom shelves. To promote stability, the heaviest items should be stored on the lower shelves as well. If your basement is wet, items that are too large to shelve such as extra furniture should be elevated off the floor. You can use packing pallets or cinder blocks—anything waterproof that raises objects above the highest water level you have experienced to date. If wood pallets do get wet, you will need to dry them thoroughly or replace them because they can mold. Labeled and sealed plastic containers work well in the basement. Make sure that labels are legible, and place labels on the sides of containers, facing out, rather than on the lids where they will not be visible if you decide to stack items.

A basement dehumidifier can help to keep dampness in check and eliminate the basement smell that mold produces. Water seepage can be controlled by installing a sump pump and French drains. A French drain is an inch-wide ditch drilled around the perimeter of your basement. Water rolls into this little crevice and then is pumped outside by the sump pump. These are not cheap solutions to a water problem, but if you have been through the trauma of losing a lot of valuables to a basement flood, you may want to consider the investment.

How to Pack to Preserve Your Stored Valuables

Books

Books should be stored spine out on shelves and supported on both sides by either bookends or neighboring books. Very large books should be stored flat. Don't pack books too tightly because this can damage the covers, and keep them out of direct sunlight and away from moisture. Books prefer a consistent temperature between 60 and 70°F and low humidity. Damp conditions will cause mold to grow, but if it is too dry, the paper can become brittle. Books need to breathe and should not be stored in airtight containers. Areas where air circulates are best. Dust can become a food source for pests, so dust books regularly as well.

Clothing

Clothing should be cleaned prior to storing. Most clothes will fare best when stored flat. Hangers can misshape and even rip fabrics over time. Fold the items, wrap them in acid-free tissue paper or clean muslin, and then place them in a plastic container. Plastic containers can promote mildew, so it is important to store only clothes that have been dried thoroughly. Include a cedar bar in the container to protect against insects. Do not store clothes in cardboard boxes. The acids in cardboard can damage clothes, and cardboard can attract bugs. Keep clothing in the dark. Direct sunlight will cause fading and even break down fragile fabrics.

Store the heaviest items on the bottom of your container, and work your way up to the lightest. An old suitcase lined with acid-free tissue paper is a great option for out-of-season clothes. Clothes fare best when stored in cool temperatures.

Photographs

A bedroom closet is sometimes the best place to store photographs. Photos need to be stored in a spot where humidity and temperature don't vary too much. Room temperature is ideal, and humidity should not run above 50 percent. Avoid dampness. Cool, dry areas are best. Black-and-white photos last longer than color photos because color prints degrade over time. If a photo is very precious, you may want to consider having a copy made to display and storing the original for safekeeping. Photos should be stored in the dark. If you can make digital copies of your family photos, you will have another way to reproduce them should anything happen to your original prints. Store prints and negatives in archival plastic sleeves, and then place these inside acid-free or pH-neutral storage boxes. Leave some space between the wall and your boxes for air to circulate. When placing photos in albums, use photo corners rather than gluing photos down, and avoid scrapbooks with magnetic pages that will ruin photos over time.

Tax Returns, Bank Statements, and Other Key Documents

Bank statements and contracts should be kept for seven years and in some cases longer. Tax returns should be kept indefinitely along with annual financial statements and stock records. If you are filing or banking electronically, back up all of these important documents so as not to risk losing them in a computer meltdown. Digital storage can be a great space saver. Both paper records and records on DVDs and the like should be stored in cool, dry areas. If you do keep a copy of your financial records on your computer, it is a good idea to protect these data by using a password to access the files.

Flammables

Gasoline, turpentine, and other flammable supplies should be stored in a locked metal container. The garage is the best spot generally, and the basement is a poor choice because proximity to the furnace and living areas can create a hazardous condition.

Small Appliances

Wrap up cords and secure them with a rubber band, and remove all batteries prior to storing small appliances. Sturdy open shelves work well. If you have the original boxes, these can provide additional protection in case of a fall or other mishap. Store the owner's manual in the same container as the appliance, tape it to the bottom of the appliance, or keep a binder in the kitchen with all your appliance manuals tucked inside.

Collectibles

Potential breakage is one of the biggest hazards to consider when storing collectibles. If there is a chance that an item may fall, wrap it carefully but loosely in acid-free tissue paper and then place it in a container lined with bubble wrap or other cushioning material. Collectibles should not be stored in direct sunlight, and if you have a lighted display case, it is best to keep the lights low. However, turning on display lights when it is damp can be a good way to cut down on the humidity in the case. Clean and handle collectibles infrequently to lower the risk that they will be broken or that acids in your skin will harm them over time. Store collectibles in cool areas with a humidity level of approximately 50 percent. Avoid extreme temperature swings, and if you relocate a fragile item, make sure to introduce any dramatic temperature changes gradually.

CHAPTER 10

Celebrating Gains and Accepting Imperfections

Quantum healing is healing . . . from a level which is not manifest at a sensory level. Our bodies ultimately are fields of information, intelligence and energy. Quantum healing involves a shift in the fields of energy information, so as to bring about a correction in an idea that has gone wrong. So quantum healing involves healing one mode of consciousness, mind, to bring about changes in another mode of consciousness.

—Deepak Chopra

Ever tried. Ever failed. No matter. Try again. Fail again. Fail better.

—Samuel Beckett

'Tis the gift to be simple, 'tis the gift to be free,
'Tis the gift to come down where we ought to be,
And when we find ourselves in the place just right,
'Twill be in the valley of love and delight.
When true simplicity is gain'd,
To bow and to bend we shan't be asham'd,
To turn, turn will be our delight,
Till by turning we come round right.

—Shaker Elder Joseph Brackett

I remember a time when my home was not the happy, well-organized place that it is now. My current career path probably has a lot to do with my memories of those darker days. I was a young wife, my daughter was just a toddler, and my marriage was in trouble. I felt completely alone, and I felt that I didn't belong anywhere. My little house perched in the Colorado mountains reflected that sentiment. In the final months before my marriage ended, both my inner and outer worlds collapsed. My home was full of chaos. So I know for a fact that our exterior lives do mirror our interior lives. I have lived through some of the same transitions that you may now face. And I've felt my life spinning out of control.

The philosophies that inform this book, such as Feng Shui and Deepak Chopra's important work on quantum healing, have demonstrated a connection among mind, body, and environment. When your environment doesn't support you, this can cause depression. If clutter keeps cropping up after you have finished reorganizing your space, the clutter may be the physical manifestation of an inner unease. If you have read the previous chapters in this book and have not yet started to make any positive changes in your own environment, you might want to ponder this connection more deeply. What is it that you are really avoiding?

There is one more important thing to consider if you are struggling to keep your space tidy after you have thoroughly assessed and organized it. Is it possible there is still some deeper disconnect in your life that you need to address? I know as soon as I get a little depressed, out comes the ratty bathrobe and the box of chocolates! Your external space is an excellent barometer of how well you are coping with the challenges in your life. Once you allow piles to reappear, it becomes even more difficult to get a positive vibe going again. Clutter is like the kudzu vine in the South. Once it takes root, it quickly overwhelms anything else in the garden. Like kudzu, clutter is an aggressive invader.

When things keep slipping into disarray at home, you can't fix the problem simply by cleaning out your closets. This is a temporary fix. To create a quantum change that will truly last, you need to envision an entirely new way of being, which is why meditation, quiet time, soul searching—whatever works for you—is so helpful. As it is said, you have to believe it to achieve it. I feel fortunate to have overcome those challenges and to now have a home that functions efficiently and supports me spiritually. However, getting to a more tranquil place involved more than just one great leap. It was a process, as it most likely will be for you. Don't be afraid to let changes unfold gradually. It took me three years to assimilate the results of my divorce, but eventually, I made a new, happier home for myself and my daughter. Be willing to give yourself the gift of time.

Losing my Colorado home along with my spouse was a devastating blow at the time. With no savings to fall back on, postdivorce circumstances dictated that my daughter and I move in with my parents. They welcomed us into their California home, but I struggled to accept their kindness. Chaos followed us to our new temporary quarters as we all tried to accommodate the piles of baby gear within my parents' three-bedroom house. I felt like a failure. I vowed that someday I would have a house again, and this time it would belong to me alone. As a single parent, earning the money I needed to support us and pay a mortgage involved sacrifice, but I ultimately managed to buy an adorable little craftsman cottage not far from my parents in the hills north of Los Angeles.

That modest house was my sanctuary, and I cherished it. I had envisioned it so many times and hoped so fervently that I would find it. To an objective viewer, it may have had many flaws, but to me, it seemed just about perfect. We were very happy there until we eventually moved on to a bigger job and a bigger home.

You may have felt just as optimistic as I did about your home when you first moved in. But over time perhaps things have devolved to a point where the house no longer works for you anymore, and that is what motivated you to buy this book. If this is the case, I hope that you've found some solace in these pages and that this book has enabled you to make the changes you need to get your life back on track. Second honeymoons are often even better than the first!

If you have already begun the process of organizing your space, good for you! Creating a space that is uniquely organized for your lifestyle is key to freeing up the positive energy in your life. A home is a sanctuary, and it should offer refuge from modern-day stresses. We all long for a sense of connectedness and belonging. By creating an active vision of your ideal room, you accomplish something life-changing. Not only do you create order in your life, but you also increase your ability to jump to the next quantum level of energy needed for further transformation. Whether you're finished organizing or just finished reading the book, you should congratulate yourself. Most people never get this far. Take a minute to review where you were before starting this book versus where you are now. Have you gained a sense of freedom? Do you have more energy? If so, savor the moment and lock it in your mind so that you can return to it if disorder begins to creep back in.

If your newfound organization starts to slip, don't beat yourself up. Review the pertinent section of this book, and attack the problem with the same dedication you had the first time around. Above all, know that you have it within your power to hold onto the gains. One of the basic premises of quantum organizing is that our systems need to evolve as lives change. Lifestyle changes can get you off track, and there will be times when a new assessment of your living space will be in order. If you add a new family member, adopt a pet, start working at home, or your youngest goes off to college, you'll need to reassess your goals and generate a new vision, at least for certain rooms in your house. You now have the organizational tools in place, so you needn't be intimidated if a room needs an overhaul. Take a few deep breaths and think about what you really want this space to embody. Then dive into "mouse view" and get to work on a new assessment. If you maintain an orderly home, all the positive energy that these new circumstances produce will be able to flow freely into your life. Think of these situations as opportunities rather than challenges, and that is exactly what they will become.

If everything in your plan is working well, there is no reason for clutter to creep back into an area. Perhaps hats and gloves are mysteriously migrating into the kitchen or newspapers are stacking up in the den. If you see piles starting to form, this may be your first clue that you need to reassess a space.

Routine maintenance is always required. There is no trick to this. The most important concept to internalize is to pick up as you go along. Although it's never as easy as it could be, with practice, it will become second nature. Resist the temptation to let messes be. Set a time each day to return things to their proper spots, and the task will never become overwhelming. If a room is organized properly, you should be able to straighten it up in just a few minutes. More important, when you return items to their places as soon as you finish using them, the job of cleaning up at the end of the day becomes even easier. Every once in a while you'll need to unclutter again. You can review the sidebars throughout this book as a guide concerning what to keep and what to give away.

If you like lists and schedules, set out what you want to review each month, and do a quick run-through of the items listed. If you are not a list person, commit to assessing a room as soon as it starts to get out of order.

Tackling piles immediately is the quickest way out of a rut and the best guarantee that you will not find yourself in that dark disorderly place again. But don't be surprised to find some old emotions in those piles you are working to eliminate. When you clear clutter from your life, you also clear clutter from your psyche. It can be momentarily off-putting as old issues crop up and need to be dealt with all over again. However, if you persevere, you will quickly feel rejuvenated by the process.

Passing It On

If there are no piles anywhere in your house, you probably feel younger and more energetic than you have in years. It's hard to beat the feeling that follows a positive leap forward. However, quantum gains can be hard to hold onto when our good intentions are thwarted by those who love us the most. Unfortunately, it may happen that the other ducks in your house don't exactly line up in a row with you. Your daughter still comes home and tosses her backpack on the first piece of furniture she encounters. You can locate your son by following the trail of dirty socks and sports equipment up to his room. Trying to maintain an orderly life when other people keep messing with your plans can seem downright impossible.

Remember that it took you a certain amount of time to make these changes in your life, and it might take your family some time to get with the program, too. If your partner, your roommate, or your kids have grown accustomed to living in a messy house, they may not even know how to pick up after themselves. It's tempting to do the work yourself rather than risk the uneven results that an "amateur" might produce, but it's a mistake to do their chores for them. Don't underestimate your loved ones. All but the very youngest children can do a few useful chores around the house. This is a time when "eagle view" comes in handy. When you ask a child to make a bed, it is not, after all, really about the bed. It is about teaching him or her to take responsibility for his or her things. A child who has had to do chores as a preschooler is more likely to adapt to the added responsibilities of school and homework than one who has never had to tackle a challenging task. And cultivating the habit at a young age makes it easier for your kids to take on more responsibility as they grow older.

If you are a list maker, you can avoid confusion during the week by giving each person who lives in your house a list of their daily or weekly chores, with specific instructions about how to do them. Rather than just saying, "Vacuum the living room," you will want to spell it out in detail, especially for children. It's not a bad idea to have your children shadow you for a few times as you demonstrate the proper way to do the task at hand. Don't be afraid to clearly define what is expected. For example, "Put all your toys away, hang up your clothes, and make your bed" is a far more helpful than "Go clean your room." After all, you can't expect family members to read your mind.

It's also essential to let children and partners adapt systems to suit their preferences. In a best-case scenario, family members have been active participants in the creation of your vision and assessment plans for the spaces that they use. Whether this is true or not, they do need to play an active role in the maintenance phase. Countless arguments arise over the "right" way to empty the dishwasher or make a bed. A little flexibility will go a long way here, and things will run far more smoothly if everyone feels included and vested in the process.

Having a set schedule for cleaning and organizing is very valuable as well. Even if you prefer a more flexible schedule, you will still want to set aside at least two times during the day, such as after breakfast and after dinner, when you go through your home room by room and put away any items that have strayed out of their zones. Kids can be encouraged to join in if you make it fun. Declare a ten-minute tidy-up time, and then reward them at the end for a job well done. Although some parents frown on rewards, they can be great motivators. In my house, a reward usually was something fun but healthy, such as being read to while sitting by the fire or going for a family bike ride. For the list makers among us, a chore chart lets kids visualize their responsibilities. If you hang the chart right above the kitchen table and children see that they are just a sticker or two away from earning a reward, you can believe they will remember to make that bed.

Keeping everyone's eyes on the prize, so to speak, is also an excellent way to attract positive growth into your life. The stronger your vision, the faster and more easily you will achieve it. Elite athletes run through their athletic routines in their minds countless times before they actually dive off the high board or perform a complicated balance beam routine. For years, coaches and trainers have recognized that detailed visualization trains muscle memory. Encourage everyone to make it a goal to stay organized, and don't be afraid to actually spend some time together as a group visualizing your home as perfectly calm and clean.

It is critical that everyone in your house (including you!) understands the importance of staying positive throughout this process. An environment filled with stress over housework will beget more stress and more housework. By focusing on what's wrong, you ask the universe to provide you with more of what you don't want. If you have followed the advice in this book and put the proper systems into place, housework shouldn't feel like a burden anymore. It will be much easier to maintain your space now that everything is in its zone and right where you need it. In time, your family will come to value how much energy they save by having supplies on hand. As soon as they start to reap the benefits, they will naturally want to continue with this process. Good quantum energy multiplies so that you become capable of achievements that seemed unimaginable before. Just as it becomes easier to stick with a diet after you've shed the first few pounds, it will be much easier for your family to hold onto the organizational gains they have made once they start to reap the benefits of a well-organized, visually appealing home. Living in a happy, calm place will extend your well-being in other realms of life as well. With all that positive energy flowing through your space, there is no stopping you.

How to Say No to New Things

One of the challenges every person faces after a quantum makeover is how to avoid refilling your nicely flowing space with new clutter. At one time or another everyone is tempted by some must-have item. Instead of allowing every new thing that crosses your path to follow you home to your living room, go back and review the assessment chapter. Ask yourself what need this new item fills and whether it is really necessary. Also, decide where its permanent place will be, and determine if there is space for it there. Last, ask yourself if you can eliminate some other item in order to clear space for your new item.

When the item is a gift, you may find it even more difficult to turn it down. However, if it really isn't something you will use, love, or save for future generations, you are probably better off saying a kind-hearted no thanks or finding another home for it.

Final Thoughts

As we've discussed throughout the book, *Quantum Organizing* is a system to empower you to take control over your clutter and regain your energy. The key to getting the most from this system is taking the time to develop the vision for your ideal space and then taking the steps to create it.

The organizing process, like life itself, is a journey not a destination. And as in life, you may encounter obstacles and setbacks along the way. You may even decide to change direction from time to time. That's okay. Acknowledge both the ups and the downs, but don't let the downs discourage you. They are just part of the landscape. Set your sights on your vision and you will always be moving in the right direction.

I wish you much success in your personal and professional life, and enjoyment every step of the way.